First World War
and Army of Occupation
War Diary
France, Belgium and Germany

5 CAVALRY DIVISION
Divisional Troops
Royal Army Medical Corps
Secunderabad Cavalry Field Ambulance
1 January 1917 - 30 April 1918

WO95/1163/6

The Naval & Military Press Ltd
www.nmarchive.com
Published in association with The National Archives

Published by

The Naval & Military Press Ltd

Unit 10 Ridgewood Industrial Park,

Uckfield, East Sussex,

TN22 5QE England

Tel: +44 (0) 1825 749494

www.naval-military-press.com

www.nmarchive.com

This diary has been reprinted in facsimile from the original. Any imperfections are inevitably reproduced and the quality may fall short of modern type and cartographic standards.

Contents

Document type	Place/Title	Date From	Date To
Heading	WO95/1163/6		
Heading	5 Cav Div Troops Secunderabad Cav. Fld Amb. 1917 Jan 1918 Apr		
Heading	141st Secunderabad C.F.A. Jan 1917		
War Diary	Bouvaincourt	01/01/1917	31/01/1917
Heading	Secunderabad 2nd. Cav. F.a. Feb 1917		
War Diary		01/02/1917	28/02/1917
Heading	Secunderabad Cav F.A. Mar 1917		
War Diary		01/03/1917	19/03/1917
War Diary	Senarpont	20/03/1917	20/03/1917
War Diary	Revelles	21/03/1917	21/03/1917
War Diary	Gentelles	22/03/1917	22/03/1917
Miscellaneous	Indian Cavalry Field Units		
War Diary		22/03/1917	23/03/1917
War Diary	Bois de Mereaucourt	24/03/1917	26/03/1917
War Diary	Halle	27/03/1917	27/03/1917
War Diary	Clery	28/03/1917	28/03/1917
War Diary	Hem	29/03/1917	29/03/1917
War Diary	Bayonvillers	30/03/1917	31/03/1917
Heading	Secunderabad Cav F.A. April 1917		
War Diary	Bayonvillers	01/04/1917	13/04/1917
War Diary	Trefcon	14/04/1917	30/04/1917
Heading	Secunderabad Cav. F.a., May 1917		
War Diary	Trefcon	14/05/1917	14/05/1917
War Diary	St Cren	15/05/1917	31/05/1917
Heading	Secunderabad Cav. F.a. June 1917		
War Diary		02/06/1917	30/06/1917
Miscellaneous	Daily State of Sick and Wounded For June 1917		
Heading	Secunderabad Cav F.A. July 1917		
Heading	Secunderabad Indian Cavalry Field Ambulance From 1st To 31st July 1917		
War Diary		10/07/1917	10/07/1917
War Diary	Trefcon	11/07/1917	11/07/1917
War Diary	Cartigny	14/07/1917	14/07/1917
War Diary	Suzanne	15/07/1917	18/07/1917
War Diary	Monchy Cayeux	20/07/1917	31/07/1917
Miscellaneous	Daily State of Sick & Wounded (Abstract) Sec. I.C.F.A. July 1917		
Heading	Secunderabad Cav F.A. Aug 1917		
Heading	Secunderabad Cavalry Field Ambulance From 1st To 31st August 1917		
War Diary	Monchy Cayeux	31/08/1917	31/08/1917
Heading	Secunderabad Cav F.A. Sept 1917		
War Diary	Monchy Cayeux	01/09/1917	30/09/1917
Heading	Secunderabad Cav. F.a. Oct 1917		
War Diary	Monchy Cayeux	01/10/1917	05/10/1917
War Diary	Stmartin	06/10/1917	06/10/1917
War Diary	Watou	07/10/1917	14/10/1917
War Diary	Bauringhem	15/10/1917	15/10/1917
War Diary	Willametz	16/10/1917	16/10/1917

War Diary	Fruges	17/10/1917	31/10/1917
Heading	Secunderabad Cav. F.a. Nov 1917		
War Diary	Fruges	08/11/1917	08/11/1917
War Diary	Montigny	10/11/1917	10/11/1917
War Diary	Morcourt	11/11/1917	11/11/1917
War Diary	Estrees En Chaussee	12/11/1917	18/11/1917
War Diary	Chuignolles	24/11/1917	30/11/1917
War Diary		01/11/1917	30/11/1917
Heading	Secunderabad F.A. Dec 1917		
War Diary	Between Villers Faucon & Lieramont	07/12/1917	31/12/1917
War Diary	Field	01/01/1918	31/01/1918
Heading	Secunderabad Ind. Cav. F.A. Feb 1918		
War Diary	Field	01/02/1918	17/02/1918
War Diary	Vignacourt	18/02/1918	28/02/1918
War Diary		01/02/1918	28/02/1918
Heading	Secunderabad Cav. F.a. March 1918		
War Diary		01/03/1918	01/03/1918
War Diary	Salouel	14/03/1918	19/03/1918
War Diary	Marseilles	22/03/1918	31/03/1918
Heading	War Diary Secunderabad C.f.a. From 10.4.18 To 30.4.18		
War Diary	Marseilles	10/04/1918	21/04/1918
War Diary	Alexandria	22/04/1918	30/04/1918

WO 95/1163/6

Secunderabad Cav. Fd. Amb.

5 CAV DIV. TROOPS

SECUNDERABAD
CAV. FLD AMB.

1917 JAN 1918 APR

Jan: 1914.

141st Secunderabad I. C. F. A

Instructions regarding War Diaries and Intelligence Summaries are contained in F. S. Regs., Part II. and the Staff Manual respectively. Title Pages will be prepared in manuscript.

Army Form C. 2118.

WAR DIARY
or
INTELLIGENCE SUMMARY

(Erase heading not required.)

224

Place	Date	Hour	Summary of Events and Information	Remarks and references to Appendices
BOUVAINCOURT 1.1.17			Took over Divisional Hospital today from MHOW I.C.F. Amb. The following transfers received. 8 B.O.R. 7 I.O.R: 1 B.O.R. admitted 9 B.O.R. 7 I.O.R. remaining. [initials]	
2.1.17			Daily sick state to noon 2nd. admitted 1 B.O.R 4 I.O.R. to ~~C.C.S.~~ Le TREPORT 1 B.O.R. remaining 9 B.O.R. 11 I.O.R. ~~All~~ British sick are transferred to LE TREPORT where they are treated as local sick. Indians are evacuated to Lucknow C.C.S. [initials] Cpl. Lewendon E A.S.C. M.T. proceeded on leave yesterday afternoon. Capt. C.S. L. Roberts R.A.M.C. proceeded on leave today. Capt. Matthews R.A.M.C. ~~to do duty~~ from 104 MHOW I.C.F.A. to do duty in this unit till the return of Capt. Johnston from leave. [initials]	
3.1.17.			Daily state to noon 3rd. admitted 1 B.O. 9 B.O.R. 1 I.O.R. (sick) to C.C.S. 1 B.O. 5 B.O.R. 5 I.O.R. remaining 13 B.O.R. 7 I.O.R. (sick) 1st Cl. Sub. Asst. Surg. ~~Pillai~~ Rajagopaul Pillai rejoined for duty from Lucknow C.C.S. yesterday. Pte 2143142 W. KELLY R.A.M.C. attached for a course of instruction in hospital duties from A.D.M.S. [initials]	

2449 Wt. W14957/M90 750,000 1/16 J.B.C. & A. Forms/C.2118/12.

Instructions regarding War Diaries and Intelligence Summaries are contained in F. S. Regs., Part II. and the Staff Manual respectively. Title Pages will be prepared in manuscript.

WAR DIARY
or
INTELLIGENCE SUMMARY

(Erase heading not required.)

Army Form C. 2118.

225

Place	Date	Hour	Summary of Events and Information	Remarks and references to Appendices
4.1.17			Daily state to noon 4th B.O.R. 5 to duty B.O.R 8 I.O.R 7 (1 venereal) remaining The new pattern portable stretcher was demonstrated today to the A.D.M.S. & G.S.O. I. 17 A.B. corps returned last evening from Secunderabad Pioneer Battalion. AWD.	
5.1.17			Daily state to noon 5th admitted 8 B.O.R. (1 malaria) (1 venereal) 3 I.O.R. to C.C.S. 4 B.O.R (1 venereal) 4 I.O.R (1 venereal) to duty 1 B.O.R (malaria) remaining 11 B.O.R. 6 I.O.R. Dr. Donovan A. TS/306 A.S.C. sent to Base H.T. depot Havre as a proposed P.B. yesterday.	AWD.
6.1.17			Daily state to noon 6th admitted 1 B.O.R. 2 I.O.R. to C.C.S. 1 B.O.R. to duty 1 I.O.R. remaining 11 B.O.R. 7 I.O.R. Dr. Law W. T/34156 A.S.C. rejoined from 7th D. Gs yesterday. Cpl. Sear F.C. remanded for court martial today charged with prejudice to good order & discipline and wilful disobedience of orders. AWD.	

2449 Wt. W14957/M90 750,000 1/16 J.B.C. & A. Forms/C.2118/12.

Army Form C. 2118.

226

Instructions regarding War Diaries and Intelligence Summaries are contained in F. S. Regs., Part II. and the Staff Manual respectively. Title Pages will be prepared in manuscript.

WAR DIARY
or
INTELLIGENCE SUMMARY
(Erase heading not required.)

Place	Date	Hour	Summary of Events and Information	Remarks and references to Appendices
7.1.17			Daily state to noon 7th	
			Sick. admitted B.O. 2 2 to C.C.S. B.O.R. 2 I.O.R 3 to duty B.O.R. 5 I.O.R 1 remaining B.O.R. 6 I.O.R. 5	
			Capt. J.C. Johnston R.A.M.C. rejoined from leave on evening of 5th AW	
8.1.17			Daily state to noon 8th	
			Sick admitted B.O. 2 B.O.R. 4 I.O.R. 1 to C.C.S. B.O. 2 I.O.R. 2 Remaining B.O.R. 10 I.O.R 4	
			Brigadier Gen. Gregory visited the hospital today & inspected the new portable stretcher. AW	
9.1.17			Daily state to noon 9th.	
			Sick. admitted B.O.R 18 I.O.R. 7 to C.C.S. B.O.R. 9 I.O.R. 3 to duty B.O.R. 2 I.O.R. 3 remaining B.O.R. 17 I.O.R. 5	
			T/15 R.A. L.Cpl. Green A.S.C. & T/23011 Dr. Swift A.S.C. proceeded on leave yesterday. AW	
			Interpreter L. G. [illegible] proceeded on leave to Paris on evening of 6th	
			M/1/08948 Pte A. Savory A.S.C. rejoined from leave yesterday. AW	
10.1.17			Daily state to noon 10th	
			Sick admitted B.O.R. 2 I.O.R. 3 to C.C.S. B.O.R. 5 to duty I.O.R. 1 Remaining B.O.R. 14 I.O.R. 7. AW	
11.1.17			Daily state to noon 11th	
			Sick. admitted B.O.R. 2 (including French Interpreter) I.O.R. 3 to C.C.S. B.O.R. 5 to duty I.O.R 1 remaining B.O.R. 14 I.O.R. 7	
			Brig. Gen. Rankin inspected new portable stretcher.	
			Kot Duffadar Abdul Rahman Khan XX Deccan Horse sick at own Duffadar proceeded to Marseilles today & return to India unfit for further service in France. AW	

2449 Wt. W14957/M90 750,000 1/16 J.B.C. & A. Forms/C.2118/12.

Army Form C. 2118.

Instructions regarding War Diaries and Intelligence Summaries are contained in F. S. Regs., Part II. and the Staff Manual respectively. Title Pages will be prepared in manuscript.

WAR DIARY
or
INTELLIGENCE SUMMARY

(Erase heading not required.)

227

Place	Date	Hour	Summary of Events and Information	Remarks and references to Appendices
12.1.17			Daily state Dhoon 12th Sick admitted B.O.R. 3 [struck out] to C.C.S. B.O.R 7 I.O.R 3 remaining B.O.R. 10 I.O.R. 4. A.D.M.S. 4th Cav. Divn. inspected the new portable stretcher today. [initials]	
13.1.17			Daily state Dhoon 13th admitted. 1 B.O. 1 B.O.R 2 I.O.R. to C.C.S. 1 B.O. 1 B.O.R. remaining 10 B.O.R. 6 I.O.R. [initials]	
14.1.17			Daily state Dhoon 14th admitted 6 B.O.R. 2 I.O.R. to C.C.S. 3 B.O.R. 2 I.O.R. to duty 2 B.O.R. Remaining 11 B.O.R. 6 I.O.R. and the following A.S.C. drivers joined for duty yesterday afternoon No T/29822 Dr. Baker F. No T/27458 Dr. Henry J. & No T3/026976 Dr. Peacock J. W. Sgt. Aylmer proceeded on leave yesterday & Sergt. Keay rejoined from leave yesterday [initials]	
15.1.17			Daily state Dhoon 15th admitted 1 I.O. 2 B.O.R. 3 I.O.R. to C.C.S. 1 I.O. 3 B.O.R. 5 I.O.R. remaining 10 B.O.R. 4 I.O.R. 1st Sub. Asst. Surg. K. Raman reported for duty yesterday afternoon [initials]	
16.1.17			Daily state Dhoon 16th admitted 1 B.O.R. 4 I.O.R. to duty 2 B.O.R. remaining 9 B.O.R 8 I.O.R.	

2449 Wt. W14957/M90 750,000 1/16 J.B.C. & A. Forms/C.2118/12.

Instructions regarding War Diaries and Intelligence Summaries are contained in F. S. Regs., Part II. and the Staff Manual respectively. Title Pages will be prepared in manuscript.

WAR DIARY
or
INTELLIGENCE SUMMARY
(Erase heading not required.)

Army Form C. 2118.

228

Place	Date	Hour	Summary of Events and Information	Remarks and references to Appendices
16.1.17			The following N.C.O & men have been awarded the Indian Distinguished Conduct service Medal.	
			No 590 Kote Duffadar KHADAR NAWAZ 26th Light Cavalry	
			691 Sowar ward orderly SIRDAR SINGH XX Deccan Horse	
			4404 Sepoy ward orderly DEVY DYAL 26th Punjabis	
			The new portable stretcher was shown today to H.R.H. Brig Gen Seely comdg Can Cav Bde. [initials]	
17.1.17			Daily state to noon 17th	
			admitted 2 B.O.R 5 I.O.R. to C.C.S. 3 B.O.R. 6 I.O.R. remaining 8 B.O.R. 7 I.O.R.	
			Dr Brown No T/29210 proceeded on leave yesterday. [initials]	
18.1.17			Daily state to noon 18th	
			admitted B.O.R. 3 I.O.R. 1 to C.C.S. B.O.R. 3 remaining B.O.R. 8 I.O.R. 8	
			Demonstrated new portable stretcher to the G.O.C. [illegible] yesterday afternoon. [initials]	
19.1.17			Daily state to noon 19th	
			admitted B.O.R. 8 I.O.R. 4 to C.C.S. B.O.R. 3 I.O.R. 4 to duty B.O.R. 1 remaining B.O.R. 12 I.O.R. 8	
			Actg Cpl. Lewindon No M1/08041 A.S.C. appointed actg Sergeant to complete War establishment of M.T. personnel.	

2449 Wt. W14957/M90 750,000 1/16 J.B.C. & A. Forms/C.2118/12.

Instructions regarding War Diaries and Intelligence Summaries are contained in F. S. Regs., Part II. and the Staff Manual respectively. Title Pages will be prepared in manuscript.

WAR DIARY
or
INTELLIGENCE SUMMARY
(Erase heading not required.)

Army Form C. 2118.

229

Place	Date	Hour	Summary of Events and Information	Remarks and references to Appendices
20.1.17			Daily state to noon 20th	
			admitted 1 B.O. 2 B.O.R. 1 I.O.R. to C.C.S. 1 B.O. 5 B.O.R. 6 I.O.R. to duty 2 B.O.R. 1 I.O.R. remaining 7 B.O.R. 4 I.O.R.	
			Court Martial promulgated today.	
			Cpl. Wheeler No M1/09276 F.C. SEAR tried by Fld Gen. Court Martial on 13th Inst. for	
			1st charge Sect. 40 when on active service conduct to the prejudice of good order & military discipline	
			2nd charge Sec. 9 (1) Army act. when on active service disobeying in such a manner as to show a wilful defiance of authority a lawful command given personally by his superior officer in the execution of his office.	
			Sentence Guilty. Verdict Reduced to ranks. One years imprisonment with hard labour.	
			G.O.C. directs that the soldier named be not committed to prison until further orders.	AWB.
21.1.17			admitted B.O.R. 4 I.O.R. 5 to C.C.S. I.O.R. 2 B.O.R. 4 to duty B.O.R. 2 remaining B.O.R. 7 I.O.R. 5	
			Capt C.S.L. Roberts R.A.M.C. rejoined from leave on afternoon of 18.1.17 and departed ~~today~~ yesterday for temporary duty with N.C.H.A. Bde.	AWB.
22.1.17			Daily state to noon 22nd	
			admitted 1 B.O.R. to C.C.S. 1 B.O.R. 2 I.O.R. remaining 7 B.O.R. 3 I.O.R.	
			No M2/191179 Pte Bankier J.W. A.S.C. joined for duty from 1st Base M.T. depot Rouen yesterday	AWB.

2449 Wt. W14957/M90 750,000 1/16 J.B.C. & A. Forms/C.2118/12.

Army Form C. 2118.

Instructions regarding War Diaries and Intelligence Summaries are contained in F. S. Regs., Part II. and the Staff Manual respectively. Title Pages will be prepared in manuscript.

WAR DIARY
or
INTELLIGENCE SUMMARY

(Erase heading not required.)

230

Place	Date	Hour	Summary of Events and Information	Remarks and references to Appendices
23.1.17			Daily state to noon 23rd	
			admitted 2 B.O. 1 B.O.R. 1 I.O.R. to C.C.S. 2 B.O. 1 B.O.R. to duty 1 B.O.R. remain 6 B.O.R. 4 I.O.R.	
			Lieut. S.K. Phadke proceeded today to join Lucknow C.F.A. for duty.	
			~~Proceeded to attend~~ attended a lecture at HESDIN today on the Eastern situation. AW.	
24.1.17			Daily state to noon 24th	
			admitted 3 B.O.R. 6 I.O.R. to C.C.S. 2 B.O.R. 4 I.O.R. to duty 1 I.O.R. remain 6 B.O.R. 6 I.O.R.	
			Received 20 beds from Brit. Red Cross Society for the hospital. AW	
25.1.17			Daily state to noon 25th.	
			admitted 3 B.O.R. 2 I.O.R. to C.C.S. 2 B.O.R. 1 I.O.R. to duty 1 B.O.R. 1 I.O.R. remain 6 B.O.R. 6 I.O.R.	AW
26.1.17			Daily state to noon 26th	
			admitted 1 B.O. 7 B.O.R. 2 I.O.R. to C.C.S. 1 B.O. 4 B.O.R. to duty 1 B.O.R. remain 8 B.O.R. 8 I.O.R.	AW
			attended a lecture on Medical services at HESDIN by Surg. Gen. Macpherson AW.	
[illegible]			Cpl. Longrove M1/08149 Pte. Weston T/26776 and Pte. Court T/35173 proceeded on leave on 23rd	
			Pte. Evans T2/016551 awarded 10 days field punishment No I for breaking out of billets without permission on 23rd Inst.	
			Bearer Arukasamy No 9213 A.B.C. rejoined for duty	
			2nd Gr. Ward Sweeper PYARAY No 5375 & No 7265 Cook JITTOO A.H.C. transferred to Lucknow C.F.A. yesterday. A/Cpl Green No T/15R/833 & Pte. Swift T/23011 A.S.C. rejoined from leave yesterday	
			Pte. Evans T2/016551 admitted to hospital & evacuated yesterday	AW

2449 Wt. W14957/M90 750,000 1/16 J.B.C. & A. Forms/C.2118/12.

Instructions regarding War Diaries and Intelligence Summaries are contained in F. S. Regs., Part II. and the Staff Manual respectively. Title Pages will be prepared in manuscript.

WAR DIARY
or
INTELLIGENCE SUMMARY
(Erase heading not required.)

Army Form C. 2118.

231

Place	Date	Hour	Summary of Events and Information	Remarks and references to Appendices
27.1.17			Daily state to noon 27th admitted 3 B.O.R. 4 I.O.R. to C.C.S. 2 B.O.R. 1 I.O.R. to duty 3 I.O.R. remain 9 B.O.R. 8 I.O.R. Qrtr Sgt. T/28081 Aylmer rejoined from base yesterday one mule evacuated to mob. Vet. Sect. yesterday. Sergt. Davis no 5714 7th Hussars proceeded for Anti gas course yesterday. [initials]	
28.1.17			Daily state to noon 28th admitted 1 B.O. 3 B.O.R. 3 I.O.R. to C.C.S. 1 B.O. 2 I.O.R. to duty 1 B.O.R. remain 11 B.O.R. 9 I.O.R. ward orderly Sepoy Dyal 26th Punjabis No 4684 & cook Ram Baran no 20 admitted to hospital yesterday Capt. C. G. J. Roberts detailed for anti gas course at Cav. Corps School commencing on 30th [initials]	
29.1.17			Daily state to noon 29th admitted 2 B.O.R. to C.C.S. 2 I.O.R. to duty 1 B.O.R. 1 I.O.R. remain 12 B.O.R. 6 I.O.R. [initials]	
30.1.17			Daily state to noon 30th admitted 2 I.O.R. to C.C.S. 1 I.O.R. remain 12 B.O.R. 7 I.O.R. Sgt. T1/2735 Williamson admitted to hospital on 28th inst.	
31.1.17			Daily state to noon 31st admitted 6 B.O.R. 1 B.O. 1 I.O.R. to C.C.S. 1 B.O. 6 B.O.R. 3 I.O.R. to duty 3 B.O.R. 1 I.O.R. remain 9 B.O.R. 4 I.O.R. A. E. Fleming Lt. Col. [initials]	

2449 Wt. W14957/M90 750,000 1/16 J.B.C. & A. Forms/C.2118/12.

Feb. 1917

Secunderabad Ind. Cav. F. A.

Army Form C. 2118.

Instructions regarding War Diaries and Intelligence Summaries are contained in F. S. Regs., Part II. and the Staff Manual respectively. Title Pages will be prepared in manuscript.

WAR DIARY
or
INTELLIGENCE SUMMARY
(Erase heading not required.)

(2)

Place	Date	Hour	Summary of Events and Information	Remarks and references to Appendices
Feb 1st 1917			Handed over Divisional hospital this afternoon to 184 MHOW I.C.F.A. Daily state to noon 1st admitted 3 B.O.R. 29 O.R. to duty 1 B.O.R. transferred to Mhow I.C.F.A. 11 B.O.R. 69 O.R. No 285 Daf. SHANKAR RAO XX Deccan Horse joined for duty as Pack Store Daffadar yesterday.	
2.2.17			No 5714 Sgt. Davis VII Hussars rejoined yesterday afternoon on completion on antigas course at Divisional school.	
4.2.17			Sweeper No 5578 MOHAN A.B.C. evacuated yesterday to Lucknow C.C.S. Pte No 5749 G. MOORE R.A.M.C. granted leave from 4.2.17 to 14.2.17 Capt. C.S.L. Roberts rejoined from corps antigas school yesterday.	
5.2.17			No M2S/3482 Pte R. BURROWS A.S.C. (M.T.) granted leave to United Kingdom from 7.2.17 to 17.2.17	
7.2.17			No 5375 ward sweeper PYARAY rejoined for duty from Lucknow C.C.S yesterday.	
8.2.17			Lieut. N.B. Aich with six bearers & 6 bearers proceeded this morning for duty with Secunderabad Pioneer Battalion. Br Sibdyal No 9226 9 Co A.B.C. promoted to acting L. Naick from 6th Jan 1917 & full Lance Naick from 6th Feb. 1917 in place of No 9121 Lance Naick AMARTH 9th Co A.B.C. reported absent from 6th Jan 1917. One water cart & two mules proceeded for duty with Secbad Pioneer battalion yesterday afternoon.	

2449 Wt. W14957/M90 750,000 1/16 J.B.C. & A. Forms/C.2118/12.

Army Form C. 2118.

WAR DIARY
or
INTELLIGENCE SUMMARY

(Erase heading not required.)

Instructions regarding War Diaries and Intelligence Summaries are contained in F. S. Regs., Part II. and the Staff Manual respectively. Title Pages will be prepared in manuscript.

Place	Date	Hour	Summary of Events and Information	Remarks and references to Appendices
9.2.17			One motor ambulance sent for temporary duty yesterday to Cavalry Corps Headquarters. D.D.M.S. Cavalry Corps visited the billets ~~yesterday~~ afternoon. AW	
11.2.17			S.P. [illegible] Mahommed admitted to hospital [illegible] 9th & discharged to duty yesterday. Pte John Jacob despatched [illegible] for return to India this morning. AW	
12.2.17			No 5578 Ward Sweeper MOHAN 9th A.H.C. died in Lucknow C.C.S. ~~yesterday~~ this afternoon.	AW
14.2.17			The sentence of one years imprisonment with hard labour awarded to M1/09276 [illegible] Cpl F. C. Sear has been suspended by the Commander in Chief	AW
15.2.17			Capt. C.S.J. Roberts R.A.M.C. reported his departure on 14 days leave today	AW
16.2.17			No 9216 Bearer Bajanath II 9th A.B.C. & No 5375 2nd Cl. Ward Sweeper PYARAY evacuated to Lucknow C.C.S. ~~today~~. yesterday.	AW
17.2.17			G.O.C. 5th Cav. Dn. inspected the ~~motor~~ transport of the Ambulance this morning along with the other Divisional Ambulances. After the inspection he informed the A.D.M.S. that it was always a pleasure to inspect the Ambulances & that they were an example to other units.	AW

Instructions regarding War Diaries and Intelligence Summaries are contained in F. S. Regs., Part II. and the Staff Manual respectively. Title Pages will be prepared in manuscript.

WAR DIARY
or
INTELLIGENCE SUMMARY
(Erase heading not required.)

Army Form C. 2118.

Place	Date	Hour	Summary of Events and Information	Remarks and references to Appendices
18.2.17			Pte J. MOORE R.A.M.C. No 5749 rejoined from leave yesterday. AW	
19.2.17			The following order was published today to the unit.	
			The Commanding Officer wishes to congratulate Sub. Conductor Terry and all the A.S.C. personnel of the horse transport on the excellent turn out at the G.O.C.s inspection on Saturday, which showed [illegible] not only that all ranks had worked extremely hard for the inspection but also the condition of the animals was a proof of unremitting care & attention. The Commanding Officer wishes particularly to record the hard work done by No T/22749 Actg Sergt. KEARY & No 9261 Bearer Sdr. ALI in getting all the carts painted in time for the inspection.	
			The G.O.C. after the march past informed the A.D.M.S. that it was always a pleasure to inspect the Field Ambulances and that they are an example to other units.	
			The Commanding Officer hopes that the high standard of efficiency that has always been maintained will continue in the future. AW	
20.2.17			Sergt. Davis & Kote Duffadar Khuda Nawaz took over charge of gas helmets & Brit. & Indian personnel respectively today.	

2449 Wt. W14957/M90 750,000 1/16 J.B.C. & A. Forms/C.2118/12.

Army Form C. 2118.

Instructions regarding War Diaries and Intelligence Summaries are contained in F. S. Regs., Part II. and the Staff Manual respectively. Title Pages will be prepared in manuscript.

WAR DIARY
or
INTELLIGENCE SUMMARY

(Erase heading not required.)

Place	Date	Hour	Summary of Events and Information	Remarks and references to Appendices
22.2.17			Sweeper No 56/T. Cherry UNGAMATTOO transferred from burden of sweeper to that of Syce.	
24.2.17			Lieut Col A. J. Flemming I.M.S. proceeded on leave to United Kingdom dated 24.II.17 to 6.III.17. Capt L. C. Johnston R.A.M.C. assumes the duties of Commanding Officer during absence of Lieut Col Flemming I.M.S. S.C.J.	
25.II.17			No 9713 3rd Gr W. Sumit Kunzly A.H.C. 7th Co arrived for duty from General India Base Depot Marseilles S.C.J.	
26.II.17			No M/08149 A/Corp Wingrove A. T/35173 Dr Court J. R. T/29210 Dr Brown J. W. T/26776 Dr Weston C. W. rejoined from leave S.C.J.	
27.II.17			Captain Maguire J. J. R.A.M.C. (SR) joined this unit for duty on 27.II.17.	
			L. C. Johnston Capt R.A.M.C.	

2449 Wt. W14957/M90 750,000 1/16 J.B.C. & A. Forms/C.2118/12.

Mar. 1917.

5

Secunderabad Cav. F. A.

Instructions regarding War Diaries and Intelligence Summaries are contained in F. S. Regs., Part II. and the Staff Manual respectively. Title pages will be prepared in manuscript.

WAR DIARY
or
INTELLIGENCE SUMMARY.
(Erase heading not required.)

Army Form C. 2118.

Secunderabad I.C.F.A. 236

Vol X

Place	Date	Hour	Summary of Events and Information	Remarks and references to Appendices
1.III.17			Took over divisional hospital this day from 104 Mhow I.C.F.A.	
			No 9216 Dr Bezenna [illegible] rejoined ~~yesterday~~ 28th to-day from Lucknow C.C.S	
2.III.17			Capt C. S. G. Roberts RAMC rejoined from leave	
			~~No~~ T/975 Dr Davis T discharged from hospital to-day	
4.III.17			No 9212 Br C Mare 93rd Coy ABC admitted & evacuated to hospital this day	
			No M3/3472 Dr Barrows R ASC rejoined from leave on 3.III.17	
5.III.17			T2/SR/02655 Dr M Quarrie R.H ASC rejoined from England & is taken on strength of unit	
7.III.17			At a parade held by divisional Commander this day the following were presented with ribbons of I.D.S.M. No 463 Sowar Ward orderly Ali Mohammed No 691 Sowar Ward orderly SIRDAR SINGH & 510 [illegible] Dafadar KHADAR NAWAZ	
8.III.17			Returned from leave yesterday afternoon. A. L. Fleming Lt. Col. IMS.	AW.
10.III.17			One horse evacuated to Umballa Mob. Vet. Sect. yesterday	
			A.D.M.S. having departed on leave Lt. Col. Fleming acts as A.D.M.S. during his absence	AW.

A5834 Wt. W4973/M687 750,000 8/16 D. D. & L. Ltd. Forms/C.2118/13.

Instructions regarding War Diaries and Intelligence Summaries are contained in F. S. Regs., Part II. and the Staff Manual respectively. Title pages will be prepared in manuscript.

WAR DIARY
or
INTELLIGENCE SUMMARY.
(Erase heading not required.)

237

Army Form C. 2118.

Place	Date	Hour	Summary of Events and Information	Remarks and references to Appendices
			Daily state of sick since 1st.	
			1st. To noon 1st.	
			transfers received from MHOW & C.F.A. 5 B.O.R. 9 I.O.R.	
			To noon 2nd admitted 4 B.O.R. 1 I.O.R. to C.C.S. 1 I.O.R. to duty 1 B.O.R. remaining 8 B.O.R. 6 I.O.R	
			To noon 3rd admitted 2 B.O.R. 1 I.O.R. (venereal) to C.C.S. 1 B.O.R (venereal) 1 I.O.R. duty 1 I.O.R remaining 9 B.O.R. 5 I.O.R.	
			To noon 4th admitted 2 B.O. 4 B.O.R. (venereal) 1 I.O.R. to C.C.S 2 B.O. 1 B.O.R (venereal) 1 I.O.R. remaining 12 B.O.R 5 I.O.R.	
			To noon 5th admitted nil to C.C.S. 1 B.O.R. duty 1 B.O.R. remaining 10 B.O.R 5 I.O.R.	
			To noon 6th admitted 1 B.O. 3 B.O.R (malaria) 1 I.O.R. to C.C.S. 1 B.O. 5 B.O.R (malaria) duty 1 B.O.R. 2 I.O.R remaining 7 B.O.R 4 I.O.R	
			To noon 7th admitted 2 I.O.R. duty 1 B.O.R 1 I.O.R. remaining 6 B.O.R. 5 I.O.R.	
			To noon 8th admitted 1 B.O. 1 B.O.R 1 I.O.R. to C.C.S. 1 B.O 2 I.O.R remaining 7 B.O.R. 4 I.O.R	

A5834 Wt. W4973/M687 750,000 8/16 D. D. & L. Ltd. Forms/C.2118/13.

Instructions regarding War Diaries and Intelligence Summaries are contained in F. S. Regs., Part II. and the Staff Manual respectively. Title pages will be prepared in manuscript.

WAR DIARY
or
INTELLIGENCE SUMMARY.
(Erase heading not required.)

238

Army Form C. 2118.

Place	Date	Hour	Summary of Events and Information	Remarks and references to Appendices
			To noon 9th	
			admitted 1 B.O.R. 7 I.O.R. To C.C.S. 1 B.O. remaining 7 B.O.R. 11 I.O.R.	
			To noon 10th	
			admitted 3 B.O.R. 4 I.O.R. remaining 8 B.O.R. 7 I.O.R. (1 measles)	
			To noon 11th	
			admitted 3 B.O.R. 1 I.O.R. To C.C.S. 2 B.O.R. 1 I.O.R. remaining 9 B.O.R. 7 I.O.R.	
			1 case of measles in XIV. Supply Col.n Mess evacuated to Le Treport	AW
	13.3.17		orders received that the Division is on 48 hours notice to move	
			one bearer No 92005 Sayannah I & one A.H.C. cook No. 4765 Latchman joined for duty from Marseilles	
	14.3.17		Lieut. N.B. Aich I.M.S. with personnel from Sec. Bad Pioneer Battalion reported for duty.	
			9198 Bearer Saminathan 9th Co. A.B. Corps evacuated to Lucknow C.C.S.	

A5834 Wt. W4973/M687 750,000 8/16 D. D. & L. Ltd. Forms/C.2118/13.

Instructions regarding War Diaries and Intelligence Summaries are contained in F. S. Regs., Part II. and the Staff Manual respectively. Title pages will be prepared in manuscript.

WAR DIARY
or
INTELLIGENCE SUMMARY.
(Erase heading not required.)

239

Army Form C. 2118.

Place	Date	Hour	Summary of Events and Information	Remarks and references to Appendices
15.3.17			Capt L. C. Johnson R.A.M.C. proceeded to Paris on leave. Dr Holmes with 1 water cart & 2 mules rejoined yesterday from S.o.c. [illegible] Pioneer battalion. 2 motor ambulances with M2-171179 Pte Bankier [illegible] & S/M/2/113256 Dr Messias S. having been evacuated to base are struck off the strength. Nos of the cars are 14670 & 14681 (Sunbeams)	AW
17.3.17			S.? Ward orderly to Raghnath Rao [illegible] Horse evacuated to Lucknow C.C.S. yesterday	AW
18.3.17			No 70325 Pte R. Clohessy R.A.M.C. joined for a course of instruction from X Battery R.H.A. today.	AW
19.3.17			A/Cpl A. L. HEARY A.S.C. No T/22749 & M2/097858 Pte T. W. Bolton A.S.C. departed this morning to their respective bases having been recalled for munition work. Orders received to move from billets tomorrow 20th inst.	AW

A5834 Wt. W4973/M687 750,000 8/16 D. D. & L. Ltd. Forms/C.2118/13.

Instructions regarding War Diaries and Intelligence Summaries are contained in F. S. Regs., Part II. and the Staff Manual respectively. Title pages will be prepared in manuscript.

WAR DIARY

or

INTELLIGENCE SUMMARY.

(Erase heading not required.)

240

Army Form C. 2118.

Place	Date	Hour	Summary of Events and Information	Remarks and references to Appendices
SENARPONT	20.3.17		The ambulance arrived at SENARPONT (15 miles) about 3.30 p.m. and billeted for the night. Only 3 motor ambulance cars available. Two being in workshops & [illegible]. Capt. T.J. MAGNER R.A.M.C. with one R.A.M.C. orderly & [illegible] to be detached for duty with [illegible] reinforcements at FEUQUIERES [illegible]. Sick were evacuated today to LE TREPORT & FRESSENVILLE.	[illegible initials]
REVELLES	21.3.17		Marched to REVELLES (20 miles) today. Arrived about 4 p.m. [illegible] ranks arriving at 7 p.m. Only 2 men fell out	[illegible initials]
GENTELLES	22.3.17		Marched to GENTELLES (17 miles). Arrived about 5 p.m. [illegible] 7 p.m. Very bad roads. A limbered wagon upset [illegible] and one Indian dislocated his [illegible] also the wagon following broke its pole. [illegible] marched very well none falling out. At a parade of Indian [illegible] the following [illegible] were [illegible] Indian Distinguished Service Medal to No 9216 B. BAGANNAH No 9236 B. LATCHMAN No 9239 B. MAHAMMAD ISMAIL No 9240 B. MAHOMMED NASSIM	

A5834 Wt. W4973/M687 750,000 8/16 D. D. & L. Ltd. Forms/C.2118/13.

List of Stores Dumped by 141st Sec'bad, 19:3:17
Indian Cavalry Field Ambce

Serial No	— Medical Stores —		No	Remarks
1	Reserve Medical Pannier		1	
2	Tool Chest		1	
3	Medical Comforts	Box	2	(1 empty)
4	Reserve Medical Comforts	"	1	
5	Surgical Pannier	"	2	
6	Clothing Bundle		2	
7	Pajamahs		6	
8	Field Medical Pannier No 2		1	
9	Bundle containing Blanket Carriers		1	
	— R.E Stores —			
1	Shower Bath		1	
2	Foot-Boards assorted		8	
	— Ordnance Stores —			
1	Tubs		4	
2	Stools, Close F.A. sets of 5		1	
3	Pans Commode		1	
4	Stretchers folding		5	
5	Lanterns G.S. Mark II		14	
6	Tables operating		1	
7	Sprayer		1	
8	Tent boards for bell tents sets		3	
9	Stove Soyers		1	
10	Pillows, Stretchers		12	
11	Saddle bag		1	
12	Stoves Canadian		1	
13	Trestles			
14	Pump, with pipe etc		1	
15	Troughs, water		1	

A. L. Flemming
Lt Col. IMS

Instructions regarding War Diaries and Intelligence Summaries are contained in F. S. Regs., Part II. and the Staff Manual respectively. Title pages will be prepared in manuscript.

WAR DIARY
or
INTELLIGENCE SUMMARY.

(Erase heading not required.)

Army Form C. 2118.

24[illegible]

Place	Date	Hour	Summary of Events and Information	Remarks and references to Appendices
22.3.17	cont^d		This award has been given for gallantry under fire. Last December these men were attached to [illegible] Pioneer Battalion and one day the party came under heavy shell fire. Everyone took shelter, but some casualties having occurred in another party these four men left their shelter without having received any orders to do so and proceeded to carry the wounded to a place of safety. One of the motor ambulances broke down this morning & had to be towed in to the repair shop. Only one motor ambulance is now left for duty. No rations received tonight. [initials]	
			Before marching from BOUVAINCOURT on 20th medical equipment as per attached list was dumped in divisional dump owing to inability to carry it on the wagons.	
23.3.17			Halted for the day at GENTELLES. The new box respirator was issued to all ranks and fitted by Gas N.C.Os. A practice with lachrymatory gas was carried out in the afternoon under the supervision of Capt. Roberts. Weather very cold. A north easterly gale with hard frost. [initials]	

A5834 Wt. W4973/M687 750,000 8/16 D. D. & L. Ltd. Forms/C.2118/13.

Instructions regarding War Diaries and Intelligence Summaries are contained in F. S. Regs., Part II. and the Staff Manual respectively. Title pages will be prepared in manuscript.

WAR DIARY
or
INTELLIGENCE SUMMARY.
(Erase heading not required.)

242

Army Form C. 2118.

Place	Date	Hour	Summary of Events and Information	Remarks and references to Appendices
24.3.17 BOIS DE MEREAUCOURT			Marched to place named in margin about 26 miles. The Indians on foot marched very well taking under 10 hours and none falling out. Bivouacked in an old German trench & dugouts. The following personnel have been detached for the purpose of treating Indians till arrival of Lucknow C.C.S.	
			To No 36 C.C.S. CAYEUX 1st S.A.S. PILLAI with 1 w. orderly 1 w. servant 1 cook 1 sweeper	
			To No 5 C.C.S. BRAY Lieut. N.B. AICH I.M.S. with 1 w. orderly 1 w. servant 1 bhisti 1 cook	
			To III corps M. dressing station PROYART 1st Cl S.A.S. N. RAMAN with 2 w. servants 1 bearer as cook 1 bhisti & 1 sweeper [?] sanitary [illegible]	
			Two motor ambulances rejoined from Repair unit.	
25.3.17			Halted for the day. A very cold day. Two Ford motor ambulances with driver No DM2/15541 ROW H. & No DM2/168177 SAMBROOK A.J. A.S.C. joined this evening. The time has been advanced one hour from today.	
26.3.17			Remained in same place under 3 hours notice.	
27.3.17 HALLE			Marched at 5.30 p.m. to marginally noted place about 5 miles. The rest of the Sec. Bde marched at 1 p.m. but through a mistake orders did not arrive for this unit till 4.15 p.m.	
			The following personnel joined: ward orderly [?] FASIHUZZAMA 27th Lr. Cav. No 1476; No MS/3181 Pte SHELDON. A.E. motor cyclist; Mason [?] SUBHANA A.B. Corps No 9262; GOURI SHANKAR — No 17463; Sweeper NACHEROO A.H.C. No MT/2040; SUKHA — MT/2062. All from ROUEN.	

A5834 Wt. W4973/M687 750,000 8/16 D. D. & L. Ltd. Forms/C.2118/13.

Army Form C. 2118.

243

Instructions regarding War Diaries and Intelligence Summaries are contained in F. S. Regs., Part II. and the Staff Manual respectively. Title pages will be prepared in manuscript.

WAR DIARY
or
INTELLIGENCE SUMMARY.
(Erase heading not required.)

Place	Date	Hour	Summary of Events and Information	Remarks and references to Appendices
CLERY	28.3.17		Marched to ~~some~~ a field just above CLERY. Very bad ground being full of shell holes & no suitable place for wagons to be parked or horses to stand. Weather changed wind going into the South. The party detached to III Corps Main dressing station on 24th rejoined in the evening. On 26th A.D.M.S. of the division visited the camp and held a parade at which he complimented the bearers lately awarded the Ind. D.S. Medal.	[illegible]
HEM	29.3.17		Marched to HEM in the afternoon, as it was supposed to be a better camping ground, but it was found to be if anything worse than the last. Very wet & cold day. The party that has been on duty at III Corps Main Dressing station rejoined the ambulance last evening.	[illegible]
BAYONVILLERS	30.3.17		Marched to BAYONVILLERS about 15 miles, and have been billeted in huts laid out as a hospital. Plenty of good accomodation both for men & horses all of which are under cover.	[illegible]
	31.3.17		The party detached for duty to 36 C.C.S. rejoined for duty ~~[illegible]~~ this evening. [illegible]	

Instructions regarding War Diaries and Intelligence Summaries are contained in F. S. Regs., Part II. and the Staff Manual respectively. Title pages will be prepared in manuscript.

WAR DIARY
or
INTELLIGENCE SUMMARY.
(Erase heading not required.)

Army Form C. 2118.

244

Place	Date	Hour	Summary of Events and Information	Remarks and references to Appendices
			Daily Sick states	
			To noon 12th 1 B.O.R. 2 admitted B.O.R. 2 to C.C.S. B.O.R. 9 1 I.O.R. 7 remaining. (returned)	
			To noon 13th 1 B.O. 1 B.O.R. admitted 1 B.O. 5 B.O.R. 1 I.O.R. to C.C.S. 3 B.O.R. 1 I.O.R. to duty 2 B.O.R. 5 I.O.R. remaining	
			To noon 14th 2 B.O.R. 10 I.O.R. admitted 3 B.O.R. 10 I.O.R. to C.C.S. 1 B.O.R. 5 I.O.R. remaining.	
			To noon 15th 2 B.O.R. 2 I.O.R. admitted 1 B.O.R. to C.C.S. 1 B.O.R. to duty 1 B.O.R. 7 I.O.R. remaining	
			16th 1 B.O.R. admitted 1 I.O.R. to C.C.S. 2 B.O.R. 6 I.O.R. remaining	
			17th 4 B.O.R. (returned) 2 I.O.R. admitted 3 I.O.R. to C.C.S. 1 I.O.R. to duty 3 B.O.R. 4 I.O.R. remaining	
			18th 8 B.O.R. 2 I.O.R. " 4 B.O.R. " 7 B.O.R. 6 I.O.R. (returned) remaining.	
			19th 1 I.O.R. admitted 4 I.O.R. to C.C.S. 7 B.O.R. 3 I.O.R.	
			20th 2 B.O. 1 I.O. 15 B.O.R. 2 I.O.R. admitted 2 B.O. 1 I.O. 22 B.O.R. 4 I.O.R. to C.C.S. 1 I.O.R. to duty nil remaining	
			21st 2 B.O. 1 B.O.R. 11 I.O.R. (2 returned) admitted ~~2 B.O.~~ 1 B. died transferred to TREPORT & FRESSENVILLE	
			22nd 2 B.O.R. 1 I.O.R. admitted & transferred to No 1 New Zealand St. Hosp. AMIENS	
			23rd 1 B.O.R. 4 I.O.R. " to 5 C.C.S.	
			24th 1 I.O.R.	
			25th 2 B.O.R. 1 I.O.R.	
			26th 2 B.O.R. 1 I.O.R. to No. 5 C.C.S. 27th 2 B.O.R. to No 5 C.C.S. 28th Nil.	
			29th 3 B.O.R. 1 I.O.R. to No 5 C.C.S. 30th ... one man of field ... sent to 36 ...	
			2 B.O. 6 B.O.R. 1 I.O.R. to No 5 C.C.S. 31st 2 B.O.R. to 36 C.C.S.	
			A. A. Clemmy Lt Col IMS	

A5834 Wt. W4973/M687 750,000 8/16 D. D. & L. Ltd. Forms/C.2118/13.

April. 1917.

9

Secunderabad Cav. F. A.

245 Vol 11

Army Form C. 2118.

Instructions regarding War Diaries and Intelligence Summaries are contained in F. S. Regs., Part II. and the Staff Manual respectively. Title pages will be prepared in manuscript.

WAR DIARY
or
INTELLIGENCE SUMMARY.
(Erase heading not required.)

Place	Date	Hour	Summary of Events and Information	Remarks and references to Appendices
1.4.17 BAYONVILLERS			Daily state to noon 1st.	
			admitted 5 B.O.R. (4 remained 1 sick) & evacuated to 36 C.C.S. CAYEUX	[illegible]
2.4.17			The hospital was opened this morning for treatment of sick of the Brigade.	
			Capt. C. S. L. Roberts R.A.M.C. took over temp. Med. ch. of N Battery & Light Sect. Am. Col. today in addition to his other duties.	
			Daily state to noon 2nd	
			admitted 1 B.O. 5 B.O.R. (1 sick) 6 I.O.R. to C.C.S. 1 B.O. 29 O.R. remaining 5 B.O.R. 4 I.O.R. (1 sick)	[illegible]
			All Indian sick evacuated to Lucknow C.C.S. established next 5 C.C.S. at BRAY	
3.4.17			Daily state to noon 3rd admitted 5 B.O.R. remaining 10 B.O.R. (1 sick) 4 I.O.R.	[illegible]
			Daily state to noon 4th admitted 4 B.O.R. 1 I.O.R. remaining 14 B.O.R. (1 sick) 5 I.O.R.	
4.4.17			2 Sunbeam motor ambulances evacuated to base today & 2 Ford ambulances received in their place. This makes 4 Ford ambulances.	[illegible]
5.4.17			Daily state to noon 5th admitted 1 B.O.R. 1 I.O.R. to C.C.S. 6 B.O.R. 1 I.O.R. to duty 1 I.O.R. remaining 9 B.O.R. (1 sick) 4 I.O.R.	
			Two Ford Motor ambulances handed over to MHOW I.C.F.A. in exchange for two ambulances.	[illegible]

A5834 Wt. W4973/M687 750,000 8/16 D. D. & L. Ltd. Forms/C.2118/13.

Army Form C. 2118.

Instructions regarding War Diaries and Intelligence Summaries are contained in F. S. Regs., Part II. and the Staff Manual respectively. Title pages will be prepared in manuscript.

WAR DIARY
or
INTELLIGENCE SUMMARY.

(Erase heading not required.)

246

Place	Date	Hour	Summary of Events and Information	Remarks and references to Appendices
6.4.17			Daily state to noon 6th	
			admitted 1 B.O. 2 B.O.R 2 I.O.R. (1 follower) to C.C.S. 1 B.O. to duty 1 B.O.R. remaining 10 B.O.R. 6 I.O.R. (2 followers)	
			Two light draught horses with harness handed over to Sec-Bad Bde Headquarters today. AW	
7.4.17			Daily state to noon 7th	
			admitted 2 B.O.R. 9 I.O.R. to C.C.S. 3 B.O.R. 5 I.O.R. to duty 2 I.O.R. remaining 9 B.O.R. 8 I.O.R.	
			One horse belonging to A.H.T. wagon evacuated to Mob. vet. sect today and one horse received from 7th D.Gs in its place	
			1 water cart and one bicycle despatched to Base yesterday as unserviceable. AW	
8.4.17			Bycee No 56 T Sherry ANGAMUTHA evacuated to A Sect Lucknow C.C.S. today	
			Brigade was put on 8 hours notice from midnight 8th/9th	
			Daily state to noon 8th – 2 B.O.R. 4 I.O.R. admitted 7 B.O.R. 12 I.O.R. (2 followers) to C.C.S. 4 B.O.R. to duty	AW
9.4.17			Daily state to noon 9th I.O.R. 2 admitted evacuated	
			Lieut Toronha I.M.S. with 1 ward orderly & a motor ambulance detached for duty with dismounted reinforcements of the division. Dr TERROTT No M/204520 A.S.C. (M.T.) joined for duty. AW	

A5834 Wt. W4973/M687 750,000 8/16 D. D. & L. Ltd. Forms/C.2118/13.

Instructions regarding War Diaries and Intelligence Summaries are contained in F. S. Regs., Part II. and the Staff Manual respectively. Title pages will be prepared in manuscript.

WAR DIARY
or
INTELLIGENCE SUMMARY.
(*Erase heading not required.*)

247

Army Form C. 2118.

Place	Date	Hour	Summary of Events and Information	Remarks and references to Appendices
10.4.17			Daily state to noon 10th 2 O.R. (1 sick) admitted ~~evacuated~~ remaining. Orders received in the evening to march tomorrow morning, but were cancelled at 10 p.m.	AWB
11.4.17			Daily state to noon 11th 1 B.O.R. 1 O.R. admitted 2 O.R. evacuated 1 O.R. 1 B.O.R. remaining	AWB
12.4.17			Daily state to noon 12th 9 B.O.R. 2 O.R. admitted 5 B.O.R. 3 O.R. to C.C.S. 5 B.O.R. remaining. Advanced dressing section paraded this morning	AWB
13.4.17			Daily state to noon 13th. B.O.R. 2 O.R. 4 admitted B.O.R. 6 O.R. 4 to C.C.S. B.O.R. 1 remaining. Received orders to march East tomorrow morning at 7.45 a.m.	AWB
14.4.17 TREFCON			Proceeded by route march to TREFCON about 20 miles and a few miles W. of ST QUENTIN. Started at 7.45 a.m. and arrived at 4.30 p.m. Bivouacked in a wood near the village. Daily state to noon 14th admitted 1 B.O.R. 2 O.R. to C.C.S. 2 B.O.R. 2 O.R.	AWB
15.4.17			A.D.M.S. visited ambulance this morning and gave instructions that all sick of the Bde are to be admitted to [illegible] who will open. This unit to remain closed. Daily state to noon 15th 1 B.O.R. admitted & transferred to [illegible] main corps dr. station	AWB

A5834 Wt. W4973/M687 750,000 8/16 D. D. & L. Ltd. Forms/C.2118/13.

Instructions regarding War Diaries and Intelligence Summaries are contained in F. S. Regs., Part II. and the Staff Manual respectively. Title pages will be prepared in manuscript.

WAR DIARY
or
INTELLIGENCE SUMMARY.
(Erase heading not required.)

Army Form C. 2118.

248

Place	Date	Hour	Summary of Events and Information	Remarks and references to Appendices
16.4.17			As the present bivouac is in the danger zone of gas attacks all ranks have to wear box respirators whenever absent from their billets.	AW
19.4.17			Orders having been received to build stables for horses material are being collected and a stable to hold 30 animals is in course of erection.	AW
21.4.17			Dr. Lewis A.S.C with one water cart proceeded for temp. duty yesterday with [illegible] train.	AW
24.4.17			The following promotions have been given in 9th Co A.H. Corps. No 9237 VELANGUNNY } to 1st Gr. ward servant - 9370 MADURANAYAGAM } - 6126 RANGASAWMY to 2nd Gr. " " - 9206 Cook David to 1st Gr. Head cook.	AW
26.4.17			The stable for 30 animals was completed yesterday. Advanced dressing section with each section, paraded this morning for an exercise. One bicycle received from base yesterday	AW
30.4.17			The following reinforcements arrived from 2nd Advanced base depot on 26th No 2825 ward orderly SAPAN SINGH (10th Lancers) No 8805 Naik PHOOBSERING 8th Co A.B.[illegible] Second cook MUNISAMY A.H. Corps.	

A. L. Fleming Lt. Col. IMS

May 1917.

5

Secunderabad Cav. F. A.

Seeibad I. C. F. A.

249

VOL XII

Instructions regarding War Diaries and Intelligence Summaries are contained in F. S. Regs., Part II. and the Staff Manual respectively. Title pages will be prepared in manuscript.

WAR DIARY
or
INTELLIGENCE SUMMARY.
(Erase heading not required.)

Army Form C. 2118.

Place	Date	Hour	Summary of Events and Information	Remarks and references to Appendices
TREFCON	14.5.17		The ambulance has remained bivouacked in the vicinity of TREFCON since 1st of month	
			Capt J J Magner R.A.M.C. & Capt. ~~L C Johnston~~ C.S.L. Roberts R.A.M.C. were on leave to PARIS from 5th to 8th	
			& Capt L C Johnston R.A.M.C. was in temporary med. charge of 7th D.G.s during the absence of Capt Magner who has been appointed to act for the M.O. absent on leave to England from 5th to 10th inst.	
			Sub. Asst. Surg. K. A. Pillai I.S.M.D. & Ward orderly Ali Md Khan proceeded for duty with dismounted reinforcements on 8th at BOIS D HOLNON and returned today.	
			Lieut. N. B. AICH I.M.S. T.C. transferred to Lucknow C.C.S. on 7th for permanent duty.	
			Sergt LEWENDON [illegible] A.S.C. admitted to hospital on 8th	
			On 11th the Army Commander presented medals to recent recipients at a parade of Sec. Bde. Among the recipients so honoured were No 9239 Br. MOHAMED ISMAIL	
			9236 - LACHMAN IV	
			9216 - BAGANAH II	
			9240 - MOHAMED KASSIM	

Instructions regarding War Diaries and Intelligence Summaries are contained in F. S. Regs., Part II. and the Staff Manual respectively. Title pages will be prepared in manuscript.

WAR DIARY
or
INTELLIGENCE SUMMARY.
(Erase heading not required.)

250

Army Form C. 2118.

Place	Date	Hour	Summary of Events and Information	Remarks and references to Appendices
16.5.17	cont^d		The weather has been very fine & hot during the month so far, with one or two days rain. Orders have been received today for the A section of the unit to go to JEANCOURT to collect casualties from the aid posts of Sec- Bde which is taking over a sector of the line in front of this place. The aid posts are about 1000 - 1500 yds away & all casualties will have to be brought back by wheeled stretchers. The [illegible] section is to move to ST CAEN and take over the main dressing station from 2/1st Midland Field Amb. of 59th Division.	
			The following equipment is handed over to S.M.O. Sec. Bde. one water cart one pr panniers with haversack & companion one haversac shell dressings 18 stretchers 100 amm. capsules	

Instructions regarding War Diaries and Intelligence Summaries are contained in F. S. Regs., Part II. and the Staff Manual respectively. Title pages will be prepared in manuscript.

WAR DIARY
or
INTELLIGENCE SUMMARY.
(Erase heading not required.)

251

Army Form C. 2118.

Place	Date	Hour	Summary of Events and Information	Remarks and references to Appendices
ST CREN	15.5.17		Took over the main dressing station at noon today from 2/1st S. Midland Fld. Amb. Capt. SNETSINGER & 11 orderlies of C.A.M.C. who was attached to this ambulance remains attached to this unit until the M.O. i/c 36 D.R. from 59th Division [illegible]. The work is very heavy for the establishment at disposal, as all the wounded & most of the sick of 59th Div. come here in addition to those of our own Bde. As Lucknow C.C.S. is closed all Indians have to be kept in this unit for the present or transferred to [illegible] I.E.F.A. AWD	
	16.5.17		Capt. MacLean R.A.M.C. with one Pte R.A.M.C. from [illegible] I.E.F.A. joined for duty. Daily state at noon 16th transfers received Sick 8 (3 diarrhoea) transfers rec'd from 2/1st Fd. Amb. admitted 2 officers 58 B.O.R. (2 diarrhoea) to C.C.S. 1 B.O. 3 B.O.R. to 2nd Rest Station 1 B.O. to Corps [illegible] 1 B.O. 1 B.O.R. Remaining 28 B.O.R. (2 diarrhoea) Wounded 3 transfers 2 admissions 5 to C.C.S. AWD	

Instructions regarding War Diaries and Intelligence Summaries are contained in F. S. Regs., Part II. and the Staff Manual respectively. Title pages will be prepared in manuscript.

WAR DIARY
or
INTELLIGENCE SUMMARY.
(Erase heading not required.)

252

Army Form C. 2118.

Place	Date	Hour	Summary of Events and Information	Remarks and references to Appendices
17.5.17			Capt. Ellis R.A.M.C. & 38 O.R. R.A.M.C. joined for duty from 2/2nd [illegible]. Capt. [illegible] & his party rejoined their unit. Lucknow C.F.A. arrived & bivouacked in vicinity. Their personnel & equipment have been placed at my disposal for duty in the hospital. The work has been very heavy for the small number of [illegible] to cope with up to now. Daily state to noon 17th - Sick [illegible] 59th D Remained 17 O.R. (2 diarrhoea) admitted 33 (2 diarrhoea) to C.C.S. 1 to D.R.S. 25 (2 diarrhoea) to C.R.S. 1 remaining 23 (2 diarrhoea) Wounded 1 admitted 1 to C.C.S. 59th D others Sick 1 transfer from [illegible] 6 admissions 7 admitted 1 to C.C.S. 5 to D.R.S. 8 remaining [initials]	
18.5.17			Daily state to noon 18th 59th D Remained 23 admitted 2 off. 28 O.R. to C.C.S. 8 to D.R.S. 5 Remaining 2 off. 38 O.R. Others Sick transfers 3 B.O.R. 8 I.O.R. remaining 8 B.O.R. (1 diarrhoea) admitted 7 B.O.R. 1 I.O.R. to C.C.S. 4 B.O.R. to D.R.S. 2 B.O.R. remaining 12 B.O.R. 9 I.O.R. (1 diarrhoea) Wounded admitted 1 I.O. 2 I.O.R. remaining [initials]	

A5834 Wt. W4973/M687 750,000 8/16 D. D. & L. Ltd. Forms/C.2118/13.

253

Army Form C. 2118.

Instructions regarding War Diaries and Intelligence Summaries are contained in F. S. Regs., Part II. and the Staff Manual respectively. Title pages will be prepared in manuscript.

WAR DIARY
or
INTELLIGENCE SUMMARY.
(Erase heading not required.)

Place	Date	Hour	Summary of Events and Information	Remarks and references to Appendices
19.5.17			Daily state to noon 19th.	
			59th Div	
			admitted sick 1 B.O. 37 O.R. to C.C.S. 5 O.R. to D.R.S. 8 O.R. to C.R.S. 2 B.O. 1 O.R. duty 5 O.R. remaining 1 B.O. 56 O.R.	
			wounded 2 O.R. 1 O.R. 2 O.R.	
			Others	
			Sick transfers received 2 B.O.R. 15 ? O.R. admitted 12 ? O.R. to C.C.S. 3 B.O.R. to D.R.S. 5 B.O.R. to duty 3 B.O.R. remaining 15 B.O.R. 24 ? O.R.	
			wounded admitted 4 ? O.R. remaining 1 ? O. 6 ? O.R.	
			[initials]	
20.5.17			Daily state to noon 20th.	
			59th Div.	
			Sick admitted 1 ? O. 41 O.R. to C.C.S. 10 O.R. to D.R.S. 36 O.R. to C.R.S. 1 B.O. remaining 1 B.O. 51 O.R.	
			wounded – 3 O.R. 1 O.R. 4 O.R.	
			Others transfers sick rec'd 5 B.O.R. 1 ? O.R. admitted 2 ? O.R. to C.C.S. 4 B.O.R. to D.R.S. 3 B.O.R. remaining 1 B.O.R. 27 ? O.R.	
			wounded 0 – 1 B.O.R. 1 B.O.R. 1 ? O. 6 ? O.R.	
			Corps troops 1 B.O. 13 B.O.R. 1 B.O. 8 B.O.R. 6 B.O.R. 11 B.O.R.	
			Capt. W. Johnson R.A.M.C. joined for duty from 2/3rd N Midland Field Amb last night. [initials]	

A5834 Wt. W4973/M687 750,000 8/16 D. D. & L. Ltd. Forms/C.2118/13.

Instructions regarding War Diaries and Intelligence Summaries are contained in F. S. Regs., Part II. and the Staff Manual respectively. Title pages will be prepared in manuscript.

WAR DIARY
or
INTELLIGENCE SUMMARY.
(Erase heading not required.)

254

Army Form C. 2118.

Place	Date	Hour	Summary of Events and Information	Remarks and references to Appendices
21.3.17			Under new arrangements all the daily states from the 6th & 5th Cav. Divs have to be submitted in future from this ambulance, as this is the only unit in which the main dressing station sick are admitted on the books. Other units inform me daily of the number of cases they have and I show them as admissions etc. By 12 noon I have to submit to the A.D.M.S. Cavalry a daily state for all Divs coming on my books & to the D.D.M.S. daily states for Cav. Corps troops & other formations. This involves 7 different states, but in the event of no patients a wire stating "nil" is all that is required.	
			Daily state for today all formations combined up to noon 21st	
			Sick: transfers 9 B.O.R. 42 O.R. — admitted 33 B.O.R. — C.C.S. 8 B.O.R. — D.R.S. 36 B.O.R. — to ambulance & C.R.S. 10 B.O.R. — duty 1 B.O. 1 B.O.R. — remaining 51 B.O.R. 31 2 O.R.	
			Wounded: admitted 4 B.O.R. — C.C.S. 6 B.O.R. — remaining 1 B.O.R.	
22.3.17			Daily state to noon 22nd	
			Sick: transfers 41 B.O.R. 82 O.R. — admitted 28 B.O. 4 B.O.R. 57 O.R. — C.C.S. 2 B.O.R. — D.R.S. 12 B.O.R. — Sub. Sect. 4 B.O.R. — C.R.S. — duty 7 B.O.R. 12 O.R. — remaining 3 B.O. 106 B.O.R. 53 2 O.R.	
			Wounded: transfers 1 B.O.R. 4 2 O.R. — remaining 1 2 O. 1 B.O.R. 10 2 O.R.	

A5834 Wt. W4973/M687 750,000 8/16 D. D. & L. Ltd. Forms/C.2118/13.

Army Form C. 2118.

255

Instructions regarding War Diaries and Intelligence Summaries are contained in F. S. Regs., Part II. and the Staff Manual respectively. Title pages will be prepared in manuscript.

WAR DIARY
or
INTELLIGENCE SUMMARY.

(Erase heading not required.)

Place	Date	Hour	Summary of Events and Information	Remarks and references to Appendices
	23.V.17		D.D.M.S. Cav. Corps visited hospital today and informed me that it was proposed to open the main dressing station nearer the line and to make ST CREN a rest station for Indians.	
			Two horsed ambulance wagons were sent to A.D.S. on 21st.	
			Daily state Noon 23rd.	
			Sick. — admitted · C.C.S. · D.R.S. · Scabies st. · C.R.S. · Duty · Remaining	
			3 B.O. 46 B.O.R. 59 O.R. · 1 B.O. 15 B.O.R. · 15 B.O.R. · 6 B.O.R. · 3 B.O. 1 B.O.R. · 5 B.O.R. 17 O.R. · 1 B.O. 109 B.O.R. 57 O.R.	
			Wounded 3 B.O.R. 2 O.R. · 4 B.O.R. ·	1 B.O. 1 B.O.R. 12 O.R.
	24.V.17		No 9281 Bearer Sher Ali appointed carpenter in place of 9267 Bearer Lutchman & Bearer No 9234 Moula Bux appointed tailor to the Indians from 15th Inst.	
			Capt. J. J. Magner rejoined from 7th C.C.S. and transferred permanently to 8th Hussars from 23rd.	
			Daily state Noon 24th	
			admitted · C.C.S. · D.R.S. · Scab. st. · C.R.S. · Died · Duty · Remaining	
			Sick 3 B.O. 63 B.O.R. 8 O.R. · 5 B.O.R. · 19 B.O.R. · 2 B.O.R. · 3 B.O. · 1 O.R. · 3 B.O.R. 5 O.R. · 1 B.O. 142 B.O.R.	
			Wounded 2 B.O. 1 O. 7 B.O.R. · 2 B.O. 2 B.O.R. · — · — · — · — · — · 2 O. 6 B.O.R. 11 O.R.	

A5834 Wt. W4973/M687 750,000 8/16 D. D. & L. Ltd. Forms/C.2118/13.

Instructions regarding War Diaries and Intelligence Summaries are contained in F. S. Regs., Part II. and the Staff Manual respectively. Title pages will be prepared in manuscript.

WAR DIARY
or
INTELLIGENCE SUMMARY.
(Erase heading not required.)

256

Army Form C. 2118.

Place	Date	Hour	Summary of Events and Information	Remarks and references to Appendices
25.5.17			The party of 2 officers and 36 R.A.M.C. lent by 59th Division were suddenly withdrawn last evening. The A.D.M.S. 5th Cav Div. arranged for one officer & 10 O.R. from Canadian Fd. Amb. to replace them but they did not arrive till this afternoon. The majority of their sick were evacuated in the evening 82 to D.R.S. & 20 to C.C.S. during the day.	
			Daily state to noon 25th	
			Sick. admitted 2 B.O. B.O.R. 59 I.O.R. 9 — to C.C.S. 2 B.O. 27 B.O.R. — to D.R.S. B.O.R. 89 — to C.R.S. B.O. 1 — to duty 12 B.O.R. 1 I.O.R. — remaining B.O.R. 73 I.O.R. 64; 2 I.O. 11 I.O.R.	
			Wounded 1 German 11 B.O.R. — 1 German 5 B.O.R. — 1 B.O.R.	
26.5.17			Capt. Ramsay C.A.M.C. & 10 O.R. C.A.M.C. joined for duty yesterday.	
			Daily state to noon 26th	
			Sick admitted B.O.R. 39 I.O.R. 4 — to C.C.S. B.O.R. 39 I.O.R. 34 — to rest camp 2 B.O.R. — duty 6 B.O.R. 3 I.O.R. — remaining B.O.R. 68 I.O.R. 31; 3 B.O.R. 2 I.O.R.	
			Wounded 7 B.O.R. — 2 I.O. 9 I.O.R. 4 B.O.R.	
			Notification having been received yesterday that Lucknow C.C.S. were open ~~for reception~~ cases were evacuated there commencing from yesterday.	

A5834 Wt. W4973/M687 750,000 8/16 D. D. & L. Ltd. Forms/C.2118/13.

WAR DIARY

or

INTELLIGENCE SUMMARY.

(Erase heading not required.)

257

Army Form C. 2118.

Instructions regarding War Diaries and Intelligence Summaries are contained in F. S. Regs., Part II. and the Staff Manual respectively. Title pages will be prepared in manuscript.

Place	Date	Hour	Summary of Events and Information	Remarks and references to Appendices
27.5.17			A site for the Main dressing having been selected close to BERNES it has been decided that this unit will move there as soon as the place can be got ready and open a main dressing station for the 4th & 5th Cav. Dns. I inspected the place with A.D.M.S. The site is a ruined sucrerie lying in a hollow. There are five Adrian huts & 3 Nissen huts but very much scattered. The roofs of the Adrian huts all leak and they are at present fitted up for and occupied by a battalion of Infantry. All the bunks in the huts will have to be removed & the roofs repaired. It is very conveniently situated for the ~~main~~ advanced dressing stations & the C.C.S. at TINCOURT.	
			Daily state to noon 27th	

	admitted	A.C.C.S.	To duty	remaining
Sick	1 B.O. 68 B.O.R.	1 B.O. 40 B.O.R.	1 B.O.R.	B.O.R. 85
	7 I.O.R.	1 I.O.R.	1 I.O.R.	I.O.R. 36
Wounded	4 Germans 10 B.O.R.	2 Germans		2 Germans
	6 I.O.R.	5 B.O.R.		8 B.O.R.
		1 I.O.R.		7 I.O.R.

Notification has been received that Pte No 9121 AMARTH A.B.C. who was reported absent last January joined 2nd Cav. Base depot from hospital on 2nd Jan. last.

WJF.

A5834 Wt. W4973/M687 750,000 8/16 D. D. & L. Ltd. Forms/C.2118/13.

Instructions regarding War Diaries and Intelligence Summaries are contained in F. S. Regs., Part II. and the Staff Manual respectively. Title pages will be prepared in manuscript.

WAR DIARY
or
INTELLIGENCE SUMMARY.

(Erase heading not required.)

258

Army Form C. 2118.

Place	Date	Hour	Summary of Events and Information	Remarks and references to Appendices
28.5.17			Capt. McLean R.A.M.C. rejoined M.V.W. ... from this unit yesterday. Daily state to noon 28th Sick. Admitted 2 B.O. 37 B.O.R. 6 I.O.R. — to C.C.S. B.O.R. 27 I.O.R. 1 — to C.A.S. 2 B.O. — to realisation 1 B.O.R. — to duty 7 B.O.R. 1 I.O.R. — remaining 87 B.O.R. 30 I.O.R. Wounded 3 B.O.R. 5 I.O.R. — 2 Germans 11 B.O.R. 6 I.O.R. — 6 I.O.R.	
29.5.17			The Battalion of Infantry (Sherwood Foresters) evacuated the barracks today and a fatigue party under Capt. Lee I.M.S. has started work on the buildings to fit them for hospital use. Daily state to noon 29 Sick Admitted 1 B.O. 49 B.O.R. 5 I.O.R. — to C.C.S. 1 B.O. 32 B.O.R. — to Sub. Sta. 3 B.O.R. — to duty 3 B.O.R. 2 I.O.R. — remaining B.O.R. 94 I.O.R. 39 Wounded 2 B.O. 4 B.O.R. 8 I.O.R. — 1 B.O. 4 B.O.R. 12 I.O.R. — 2 I.O.R. AWR.	

A5834 Wt. W4973/M687 750,000 8/16 D. D. & L. Ltd. Forms/C.2118/13.

Instructions regarding War Diaries and Intelligence Summaries are contained in F. S. Regs., Part II. and the Staff Manual respectively. Title pages will be prepared in manuscript.

WAR DIARY
or
INTELLIGENCE SUMMARY.
(Erase heading not required.)

259

Army Form C. 2118.

Place	Date	Hour	Summary of Events and Information	Remarks and references to Appendices
30.5.17			Daily state to noon 30th	
			Sick — Admitted: 47 B.O.R., 4 ?.O.R. — To C.C.S: 23 B.O.R., 8 ?.O.R. — To rest stn: 3 B.O.R. — To duty: 9 B.O.R. — Remaining: 106 B.O.R., 35 ?.O.R.	
			Wounded — Admitted: 1 B.O. 1 B.O.R., 5 ?.O.R. — To C.C.S: 1 B.O., 1 B.O.R. 5 ?.O.R. — Remaining: 2 ?.O.R.	
			ALF	
31.5.17			Daily state to noon 31st.	
			Sick — Admitted: B.O.R. 37 ?.O.R. 5 — To C.C.S: 29 B.O.R., 3 ?.O.R. — To rest stn: 4 B.O.R. — To duty: 15 B.O.R., 2 ?.O.R. — Remaining: 96 B.O.R., 35 ?.O.R.	
			Wounded — Admitted: 1 B.O., 4 B.O.R., 2 ?.O.R. — To C.C.S: 1 B.O., 4 B.O.R., 2 ?.O.R. — Remaining: 2 ?.O.R.	
			A. L. Fleming Lt Col RAMC	

A5834 Wt. W4973/M687 750,000 8/16 D. D. & L. Ltd. Forms/C.2118/13.

June. 1917.

Secunderabad Cav. F. A.

Instructions regarding War Diaries and Intelligence Summaries are contained in F. S. Regs., Part II. and the Staff Manual respectively. Title pages will be prepared in manuscript.

WAR DIARY
or
INTELLIGENCE SUMMARY.
(Erase heading not required.)

Army Form C. 2118.

260

Place	Date	Hour	Summary of Events and Information	Remarks and references to Appendices
2.6.17			Moved to Suzanne N of BERNES with the tent section of this unit, and opened a main dressing station for the 4th & 5th Cav Dns.	
			Dr. THORPE ASC proceeded on leave yesterday.	
			No 9255 Bearer Lutchmun 4259 – Lachman III } transferred sick to Lucknow C.C.S MT 2062 Sweeper Sukha	AMS
3.6.17			Capt. Quinn RAMC Lt. Narayan IMS with 4 B.O.R & 34 I.O.R (including 1 S.A.S) from SIALKOTE C.F.A. joined for duty today. Working very hard to get the hospital in order for patients and at the same time receiving sick & wounded	AMS
6.6.17			Capt Hunt C.A.M.C. and 12 O.R. from Canadian C.F.A. joined for duty yesterday	AMS
8.6.17			10 wounded Indians admitted yesterday. AMS	

A5834 Wt. W4973/M687 750,000 8/16 D. D. & L. Ltd. Forms/C.2118/13.

Instructions regarding War Diaries and Intelligence Summaries are contained in F. S. Regs., Part II. and the Staff Manual respectively. Title pages will be prepared in manuscript.

WAR DIARY
or
INTELLIGENCE SUMMARY.
(Erase heading not required.)

Army Form C. 2118.

261

Place	Date	Hour	Summary of Events and Information	Remarks and references to Appendices
	13.6.17		22 Indian wounded admitted to day, most of them from 20th Deccan Horse. The majority were slight cases, bomb wounds	[illegible]
	15.6.17		26 Indian wounded admitted to day mostly from 19th Lancers. The majority were slight cases.	[illegible]
	16.6.17		D.D.M.S. Cavalry Corps inspected the hospital this morning & expressed his pleasure at the arrangements generally.	[illegible]
	18.6.17		A.D.M.S. 2nd Cav Div visited the hospital today with one of his Ambulance C.Os	[illegible]
	30.6.17		During the month the main dressing station has passed through its books 68 B.O.R & 141 I.O.R wounded, some of which however were transferred direct to C.C.S. from A.D.S. And 736 B.O.R and 230 I.O.R have passed through the books as sick. Of these however large numbers have been treated in other medical units of 4th & 5th Cav Divns notably in M.H. on I.C.F.A. ~~[illegible]~~ but these numbers practically are the actual numbers of sick admitted in these two divisions during the month as this unit is the only one that keeps an A&D book, but an allowance must be made for other formations e.g. corps troops labour companies etc which reduce the real admissions from these two divisions considerably. The D.D.M.S. Cav Corps visited the M.D.S. again on 29th inst	Table of admissions discharges etc attached

A5834 Wt. W4973/M687 750,000 8/16 D. D. & L. Ltd. Forms/C.2118/13.

Army Form C. 2118.

Instructions regarding War Diaries and Intelligence Summaries are contained in F. S. Regs., Part II. and the Staff Manual respectively. Title pages will be prepared in manuscript.

WAR DIARY
or
INTELLIGENCE SUMMARY.
(Erase heading not required.)

262

Place	Date	Hour	Summary of Events and Information	Remarks and references to Appendices
	30.6.17 (cont).		The following A S C personnel have joined	
			T/3/029898 Dr. J Stuckworth } on 17th	
			T/17668 " J Cox }	
			T3/024496 Dr. E. Aldridge on 27th	
			and No T1/1759 Dr. S. Bailey evacuated sick on 21st	
			Actg. 2/Cpl Green appointed Cpl. acting pay & Dr Taylor No T1/1873 [illegible] appointed actg 2/Cpl. without pay on 19th.	
			L/Cpl. Tapsell & Dr Sawson proceeded on leave to England	
			A kit inspection held during the month	
			No 9793 B. Salumathan joined today for duty in exchange for Bearer No 5190 [illegible] sent to Sialkote C F A	
			Baths carried out regularly.	
			A concert was held on 20th.	
			A. L. Fleming Lt. A.S.C. [illegible]	

A5834 Wt. W4973/M687 750,000 8/16 D. D. & L. Ltd. Forms/C.2118/13.

Daily State of Sick and Wounded for June 1917

		Admitted				To C.C. Stn.				To D. R Stn.				To C R Stn.				To duty				Remaining			
		BO	IO	BOR	IOR	BO	IO	BOR	IOR	BO	IO	BOR	IOR	BO	IO	BOR	IOR	BO	IO	BOR	IOR	BO	IO	BOR	IOR
Daily State up to noon 1st June	SICK	-	-	39	7	-	-	38	3	-	-	-	-	-	-	-	-	-	-	13	3	-	-	84	36
	WOUNDED	-	-	3	2	-	-	2	-	-	-	-	-	-	-	-	-	-	-	-	-	-	-	1	4
" " up to noon 2nd June	SICK	-	-	15	10	-	-	22	8	-	-	-	-	-	-	4	-	-	-	8	2	-	-	65	36
	WOUNDED	-	-	5	2	-	-	4	2	-	-	-	-	-	-	-	-	-	-	2	-	-	-	-	4
" " " " 3rd June	SICK	-	-	14	4	-	-	3	1	-	-	30	29	-	-	-	-	-	-	2	1	-	-	44	9
	WOUNDED	1	1	-	6	1	1	-	10	-	-	-	-	-	-	-	-	-	-	-	-	-	-	-	-
" " 4th June	SICK	1	-	29	6	1	-	10	1	-	-	9	1	-	-	-	-	-	-	-	-	-	-	52	13
	WOUNDED	-	-	3	3	-	-	1	2	-	-	-	-	-	-	-	-	-	-	2	1	-	-	-	-
" " 5th June	SICK	1	-	22	10	1	-	7	8	-	-	10	-	-	-	2	-	-	-	12	-	-	-	43	15
	WOUNDED	-	-	-	4	-	-	-	4	-	-	-	-	-	-	-	-	-	-	-	-	-	-	-	-
" " 6th June	SICK	3	-	24	10	3	-	3	2	-	-	6	1	-	-	1	-	-	-	1	-	-	-	56	22
	WOUNDED	-	-	2	-	-	-	2	-	-	-	-	-	-	-	-	-	-	-	-	-	-	-	-	-
" " 7th June	SICK	1	-	26	7	1	-	8	-	-	-	7	3	-	-	4	-	-	-	7	-	-	-	56	26
	WOUNDED	-	-	3	10	-	-	1	2	-	-	-	-	-	-	-	-	-	-	-	-	-	-	2	8
" " 8th June	SICK	-	-	36	12	-	-	6	8	-	-	1	-	-	-	3	-	-	-	4	5	-	-	78	25
	WOUNDED	-	-	4	-	-	-	5	8	-	-	-	-	-	-	-	-	-	-	-	-	-	-	1	-
" " 9th June	SICK	3	1	26	6	1	-	6	4	1	-	8	6	-	-	2	-	-	-	7	2	1	1	81	19
	WOUNDED	-	-	3	-	-	-	1	-	-	-	-	-	-	-	-	-	-	-	-	-	-	-	3	-
" " 10th June	SICK	2	1	19	1	2	1	11	1	1	-	13	-	-	-	-	-	-	-	9	-	-	1	67	19
	WOUNDED	2	-	6	3	2	-	6	1	-	-	-	-	-	-	-	-	-	-	-	-	-	-	3	2
" " 11 June	SICK	2	-	32	6	1	-	4	2	-	-	12	-	-	-	2	-	-	-	8	-	1	1	73	23
	WOUNDED	1	-	1	5	1	-	1	7	-	-	-	-	-	-	-	-	-	-	-	-	-	-	3	-
" " 12 June	SICK	1	-	24	8	2	-	4	4	-	-	4	4	-	-	-	-	-	-	8	-	-	1	81	23
	WOUNDED	1	-	1	6	1	-	1	2	-	-	1	-	-	-	-	-	-	-	-	3	-	-	2	1
" " 13 June	SICK	2	-	18	8	-	-	2	5	-	-	23	1	1	-	-	-	-	-	3	-	1	1	71	25
	WOUNDED	3	1	2	22	1	-	-	4	-	-	1	-	-	-	-	-	-	-	-	-	2	1	3	18
" " 14 June	SICK	1	-	21	5	1	-	8	1	-	-	11	8	-	-	4	-	-	-	3	-	1	1	66	21
	WOUNDED	2	-	2	8	3	1	1	14	-	-	-	-	-	-	-	-	-	-	-	-	1	-	4	12
" " 15 June	SICK	1	-	22	13	1	-	1	3	-	-	6	7	-	-	2	-	-	-	-	1	1	1	79	23
	WOUNDED	1	1	1	26	2	1	1	13	-	-	-	-	-	-	-	-	-	-	-	-	-	-	4	25
" " 16th June	SICK	1	-	30	4	2	-	9	5	-	-	12	1	-	-	1	-	-	1	11	-	-	-	76	21
	WOUNDED	-	-	4	5	-	-	3	19	-	-	-	-	-	-	-	-	-	-	2	1	-	-	3	10
" " 17 June	SICK	2	-	20	11	-	-	5	4	-	-	4	2	-	-	-	-	-	-	11	2	2	-	76	24
	WOUNDED	-	-	2	5	-	-	1	-	-	-	1	-	-	-	-	-	-	-	1	-	-	-	2	15
" " 18 June	SICK	1	-	18	4	3	-	5	1	-	-	6	3	-	-	1	-	-	-	4	-	-	-	78	24
	WOUNDED	-	-	2	2	-	-	3	5	-	-	-	4	-	-	-	-	-	-	1	-	-	-	-	8
" 19th –	SICK			29	2			11	1			6	8			5				5	7			80	12
	WOUNDED			1	4							1	8								1				4
– 20 –	SICK	2		36	20	2		7	11			7	-							9				93	27
	WOUNDED			57	5			2	1												2			2	6
21st	SICK	1		25	13	1		7	3			17	12			1				7				86	19
	WOUNDED							1												1				-	6
22nd –	SICK	1	1	24	11	1		7	1	1		12	3							9			1	82	26
	WOUNDED			4	1																			4	5
23rd –	SICK	1	1	18	7	1		5	2			7	3							4			2	84	26
	WOUNDED	1	[illegible]	6		1	[illegible]	7	1				3											3	1
24th –	SICK			23	6			9	8			16	4			1				11			1	70	18
	WOUNDED				1																			3	2
25th	SICK			24	1		1	4	5			8				1				8				73	14
	WOUNDED				1			3																	3
26th	SICK	4		26	5	4		10				8				1				12				68	19
	WOUNDED			1	2			1	1																4
27th	SICK			19	5			5	3			5	2			1				5	2			71	17
	WOUNDED	1		1	3				3									1						1	4
28	SICK	1		17	3	1		6				12				1				4	1			65	19
	WOUNDED	1		1	12	1		1	6												1			1	9
29	SICK			28	12			5				15	5			1				3	2			69	28
	WOUNDED	1																1							6
	SICK			29	13			7	8			7	11			1				2	1			81	12
	WOUNDED			3	3				4															3	5

1 died

July 1917

Secunderabad Cav. F.A.

"Medical."

Serial No: 248.

Secunderabad Indian Cavalry Field Ambulance.

From 1st to 31st July 1917.

Instructions regarding War Diaries and Intelligence Summaries are contained in F. S. Regs., Part II. and the Staff Manual respectively. Title pages will be prepared in manuscript.

WAR DIARY
or
INTELLIGENCE SUMMARY.
(Erase heading not required.)

Army Form C. 2118.

263

Place	Date	Hour	Summary of Events and Information	Remarks and references to Appendices
10.7.17			The Main Dressing Station was handed over today to 102nd Field Ambulance, and the unit marched to Bivouac in TREFCON. The following complimentary order was issued "The Officer Commanding wishes to express his appreciation of the work done by all ranks during the time this unit has been open as a Main Dressing Station. Inspecting officers have frequently commented very favourably on the hospital and such praise has been earned on account of the keenness of the hospital staff & personnel. The Officer Commanding wishes particularly to thank the personnel who have been attached from the Canadian & Sialkot Cav. Fd. Ambulances whose assistance has been invaluable."	
			E.f.I. Army orders [illegible] 6769 d/9th May 1917 extract. No 1390 1st Sub. Asst. Surg. Culpankam Virasami [illegible] Pillai to be 2nd cl. Sen. Sub. Asst. Surg. ranking as Jemadar on [illegible] of 15 years service [illegible] 31st March 1921	

A5834 Wt. W4973/M687 750,000 8/16 D. D. & L. Ltd. Forms/C.2118/13.

Instructions regarding War Diaries and Intelligence Summaries are contained in F. S. Regs., Part II. and the Staff Manual respectively. Title pages will be prepared in manuscript.

WAR DIARY
or
INTELLIGENCE SUMMARY.
(Erase heading not required.)

Army Form C. 2118.

264

Place	Date	Hour	Summary of Events and Information	Remarks and references to Appendices
10.7.17 contd.			Extr. from Ambulance orders of 5.7.17 The G.O.C. 5th Cav. Dn. has remitted the sentence of one years rigorous imprisonment passed on 18th Jan 1917 on No 1/59276 Driver Sear, T.C. as follows – "I have reconsidered the sentence and hereby remit it. sd H. J. M. Macandrew Maj General 5th Cav. Dn." Lieut. F. H. Noronha proceeded on 14 days leave to England on 7.7.17	
TREFCON 11.7.17			The following ~~letter~~ has been received & published to all concerned. Extr. from a letter received from Maj Gen. Comdg 5th Cav. Dn. by A.D.M.S. 5th Cav. Dn. "Having come out of the line, I take the opportunity of thanking you and all under you for the very efficient ~~way~~ work both you & they have performed all the time we have been taking part in active operations. All has been most carefully thought out, and after experience with a good many divisions in the war I have no hesitation in saying that the wounded of the 5th Cav. Dn. have a great deal to be thankful for. As you know the medical arrangements of the division have been held up as an example to other divisions. Please inform Lt. Col. Fleming & Maj. Matthews how very satisfactory their work has been."	

A5834 Wt. W4973/M687 750,000 8/16 D. D. & L. Ltd. Forms/C.2118/13.

Instructions regarding War Diaries and Intelligence Summaries are contained in F. S. Regs., Part II. and the Staff Manual respectively. Title pages will be prepared in manuscript.

WAR DIARY
or
INTELLIGENCE SUMMARY.
(Erase heading not required.)

265 Army Form C. 2118.

Place	Date	Hour	Summary of Events and Information	Remarks and references to Appendices
11.7.17 Cont'd			Extr. from reply to above dated 10th July 1917 On behalf of Field Ambulance Commanders, the medical establishment of the division generally & on my own I wish to thank you very much for so high an appreciation of the work that has been done by them during the time that the division has been taking part in active operations, and I know how much pleasure the communication of your kind remarks will give them. I feel sure that I express the feeling of all Medical Officers of the division when I say that we well recognise the privilege of serving in it and are prepared to do all that is possible on our part to assist in maintaining its reputation & efficiency	
12.7.17 CARTIGNY			Moved by route march to CARTIGNY today under orders of S.O.C. [illegible] and bivouacked at COURCELLES for the night.	[illegible]
15.7.17 SUZANNE			Moved by route march to SUZANNE and bivouacked for the night.	

A5834 Wt. W4973/M687 750,000 8/16 D. D. & L. Ltd. Forms/C.2118/13.

Instructions regarding War Diaries and Intelligence Summaries are contained in F. S. Regs., Part II. and the Staff Manual respectively. Title pages will be prepared in manuscript.

WAR DIARY
or
INTELLIGENCE SUMMARY.
(Erase heading not required.)

Army Form C. 2118.

266

Place	Date	Hour	Summary of Events and Information	Remarks and references to Appendices
16.7.17			Moved by route march to MORLANCOURT and bivouacked for the night	
17.7.17			— — — MARIEUX	
18.7.17			— — — ST POL and eventually [illegible] at ROSEMONT. A long march of 20 miles. Left at 6.15 a.m. and reached bivouac at about 3 p.m.	
MONCHY CAYEUX 20.7.17			Owing to the distance of water for animals the Brigade moved to a new area and the ambulance changed its bivouac to the vicinity of MONCHY CAYEUX	
			The following awards have been made	
			Meritorious service medal (London Gazette 9th July 1917)	
			Sub conductor C E TERRY S&T Corps	
			Indian Meritorious service medal ([illegible] 14th July 1917)	
			Indian Sub Med department	
			No 1289 1st Cl Sub Asst Surg KUNNIYAL ASSAN	
			1390 " " CULPANKAM VIRASAMI RANGA PAUL PILLAI	
			Army Hosp. Corps No 9248 1st Grade ward servant KAILASUM [illegible]	

A5834 Wt. W4973/M687 750,000 8/16 D. D. & L. Ltd. Forms/C.2118/13.

Instructions regarding War Diaries and Intelligence Summaries are contained in F. S. Regs., Part II. and the Staff Manual respectively. Title pages will be prepared in manuscript.

WAR DIARY
or
INTELLIGENCE SUMMARY.
(Erase heading not required.)

267

Army Form C. 2118.

Place	Date	Hour	Summary of Events and Information	Remarks and references to Appendices
31.7.17			No 749 Pte G. Moore R.A.M.C. proceeded for duty with headquarters 5th Cav. Bde in exchange with No 43653 Pte T. Lunn [?] R.A.M.C. on 19th.	
			Lieut F. H. Noronha I.M.S. rejoined from leave on 23rd.	
			7 men of A.S.C. have been granted leave to England 3 on 23rd & 4 on 28th.	
			Pte E Aldridge No T2/024496 A.S.C. awarded 14 days C.C. for failing to comply with an order on 25.7.17.	
			Capt D. Ross R.A.M.C. (T.C.) joined the ambulance for duty on 29.7.17 from No 11 Stationery hospital	
			A. H. Fleming Lt Col. I.M.S.	

Daily State of Sick & wounded (Abstract) Sec. 9. C.F.A. July 1917

		Admitted				C.C.St.				D.R.St.				C.R.St.				Duty								Remained			
		BO	IO	BOR	IOR	BO	IO	BOR	IOR	BO	IO	BOR	IOR	BO	IO	BOR	IOR	BO	IO	BOR	IOR	BO	IO	BOR	IOR	BO	IO	BOR	IOR
30 to 1	Sick	2		27	7	2		6	1			16	1				-			9	-					/		78	21
	Wd			3	1			3	3			-	-											1'				2	3
1 to 2	Sick			24	9			10	5			6	-			2	-			12	2							72	23
	Wd			28	-			24	1			6	-																1
2 - 3	Sick	1	0	16	3	1		8	2			12	4				-			5	-			1	3			63	17
	Wd			10	10			2	5			-					-			2	-			1[xx]	3[xx]			5	4
3 - 4	Sick	1	1	33	9	1		12	3			7	4							3	2		1	73	17
	Wd			1	1			3	-			2	1							-	-							1	4
4 - 5	Sick		1	27	9			6	6			15	2			1	-			2	2						1	74	15
	Wd			2	3			1	3			-									1							2	3
5 - 6	Sick			19	10[x]			6	10			8	-			1	-			7							1	73	15
	Wd			1	2[x]			3	3			-	-															1	2
6 - 7	Sick	2[x]		16	5[o]	2		10	4			6				2				9	2						1	62	14
	Wd			2[x]	-			1	-			-				1				1	-							1	2
7 - 8	Sick			21[x]	6[x]		1	9	5			4				1				3	1			1[o]	1[xx]			65	14
	Wd			6[x]	7			2	6			1								1	1							2	1
8 - 9	Sick	3		21[x]	1	3		8	-			8	4							14	-							52	11
	Wd	4	4	29	8[x]		2	10	6			1	-					3	2	3	2			1[A]				17	-
9 - 10	Sick	1		16	3	1		14	3			11	2			3[E]				14	8			6[A] 2[B] 17[C] 3[D]	1[A]			-	-
	Wd			10	-			8	-			10	-							5	0			4[C]				-	-
13 - 14	Sick			2[E]	2			1[E]				1	2						-		-							-	-
	Wd			-	-			-												-	-			-	-			-	-

x Includes Transfers received
° 41 Stationary Hospl. Gailly.
xx Died

A Transferred to Mhow C.F.A.
B —"— Canadian —"—
C —"— 102nd Fld. Amb. 34 Div.
D Evacuated to 42 Stationary Hospl. Amiens
E Includes French Interpreter

Aug 1917
I

Secunderabad Cav. F.A.

"Medical".

Serial No: 248.

Secunderabad Cavalry Field Ambulance.

From 1st to 31st August 1917.

Instructions regarding War Diaries and Intelligence Summaries are contained in F. S. Regs., Part II. and the Staff Manual respectively. Title pages will be prepared in manuscript.

SEC BAD I.C.F.A.

WAR DIARY
or
INTELLIGENCE SUMMARY.

(*Erase heading not required.*)

268

Army Form C. 2118.

Place	Date	Hour	Summary of Events and Information	Remarks and references to Appendices
MONCHY CAYEUX	31.8.17		During the month the unit has not changed its location, but has remained in billets of Nissen huts at MONCHY CAYEUX. It has remained closed during the whole month the sick of the Sec Bad Bde being collected daily and sent into MHOW I.C.F.A. who have been open. The weather on the whole has been very bad, storms and rain prevailing. A divisional horse show was held on 15th. G.O.C. Division inspected the ambulance along with the Sec Bad Bde on 20th. Baths & parades. The pack mounted section has paraded on several occasions during the month under Capt L.C. Johnston R.A.M.C. The A.B. Corps & followers have had daily drills, and a route march on 3 days a week. The following officers have been on leave. Capt L.C. Johnston 12th to 22nd Capt C.S.L. Roberts 22nd to 1st Sept. also Sergt Maj W Robertson R.A.M.C and 24 other ranks.	

Instructions regarding War Diaries and Intelligence Summaries are contained in F. S. Regs., Part II. and the Staff Manual respectively. Title pages will be prepared in manuscript.

WAR DIARY
or
INTELLIGENCE SUMMARY.
(Erase heading not required.)

Army Form C. 2118.

269

Place	Date	Hour	Summary of Events and Information	Remarks and references to Appendices
			I acted as A.D.M.S. of the Division for 10 days during the absence of Col. G. J. Macnab IMS on leave.	
			Reinforcements.	
			Capt. D. Ross R.A.M.C. joined on 29.7.17	
			Lieut. E. S. Orvicup M.O.R.C. U.S.A. joined on 23.8.17	
			No 8362 Bearer Ram Barose 8th Coy A.B.C.	
			" 3572 " Jiwan 3rd " "	19.8.17
			" 13143 " Lachman Singh " "	
			No 6708 Ward Servant Changor Rama Mahin 6 Coy A.H.C.	
			Wastage. No 8277 Br Shamram 8th Coy A.B.C. was evacuated sick to Lucknow C.C.S. on 17.8.17	
			Capt. D. Ross R.A.M.C. proceeded for temporary duty with R.H.A. H.Q. on 16.8.17	

A5834 Wt. W4973/M687 750,000 8/16 D. D. & L. Ltd. Forms/C.2118/13.

Army Form C. 2118.

WAR DIARY
or
INTELLIGENCE SUMMARY.
(Erase heading not required.)

270

Instructions regarding War Diaries and Intelligence Summaries are contained in F. S. Regs., Part II. and the Staff Manual respectively. Title pages will be prepared in manuscript.

Place	Date	Hour	Summary of Events and Information	Remarks and references to Appendices
			The following personnel & medical equipment proceeded to Cavalry Remount depot near BAILLEUL on 18.8.17. Lieut. F H Noronha I.M.S. 1st Cl. Sub Asst Surg. Rasagopaul Pillai Pte. T. Lunn R.A.M.C. Bearer George Ward Orderly Fazruddin Cook Ram Baroo Sweeper Thumboosamy with one pair field med panniers one Fd. Med. Companion & one surg haversack to take medical charge & also treat any Indian sick in a casualty clearing station should this be necessary. Orders have been received for Capt C.S. L Roberts R.A.M.C. to proceed to No 5 Convalescent depot on his return from leave.	

A5834 Wt. W4973/M687 750,000 8/16 D. D. & L. Ltd. Forms/C.2118/13.

Instructions regarding War Diaries and Intelligence Summaries are contained in F. S. Regs., Part II. and the Staff Manual respectively. Title pages will be prepared in manuscript.

WAR DIARY
or
INTELLIGENCE SUMMARY.
(Erase heading not required.)

271

Army Form C. 2118.

Place	Date	Hour	Summary of Events and Information	Remarks and references to Appendices
			Interpreter Fargues returned off leave on 4 8 17 and proceeded to 1st Army Headquarters for duty the same day. Interpreter Vermignon returned from leave on 10 8 17 and proceeded for duty to the American Mission on 20 8 17. Punishments. No 1/4 / 234371 Pte Cowdery W. 10 days C.C. on 18 8 17 "Making an improper reply to a warrant officer" No I / 29822 Pte Baker H. 14 days C.C. on 14 8 17 Turning out dirty on a F.O.C. parade No I / 34673 Pte Sanson J. 14 days C.C. on 21 8 17 Speaking in a disrespectful manner to N.C.O. Two sweepers from Sanitary section reported for temporary duty on 30 8 17	

A5834 Wt. W4973/M687 750,000 8/16 D. D. & L. Ltd. Forms/C.2118/13.

272

Army Form C. 2118.

WAR DIARY
or
INTELLIGENCE SUMMARY.
(Erase heading not required.)

Instructions regarding War Diaries and Intelligence Summaries are contained in F. S. Regs., Part II. and the Staff Manual respectively. Title pages will be prepared in manuscript.

Place	Date	Hour	Summary of Events and Information	Remarks and references to Appendices
			Wheeler F. Sear No M1 09276 proceeded ~~from~~ on 22.8.17 for temporary duty with 5th Cav. A.H.T. Coy	
			One charger received ~~from~~ on 12.8.17	
			One riding horse transferred to M.H.O.W. D. F. A. on 29.8.17 received from base on 31.8.17	
			Pte No 7822 R. W. McNeil R.A.M.C. transferred for duty to 5th Cav. Dn. Reserve Park on 25.8.17 in exchange for Pte W. Bartonwood R.A.M.C. No 40183	
			Two motor cycles (in replacement of others dispatched to base out of order) were received on 21.8.17 & 27.8.17	
			A. L. Fleming Lt Col. IMS	

A5834 Wt. W4973/M687 750,000 8/16 D. D. & L. Ltd. Forms/C.2118/13.

Sept. 1917

Second Lond. Cas. F.A.

Secunderabad Cavalry Field Ambulance. "Medical" Secbad C.F.A 273

Army Form C. 2118.

WAR DIARY
or
INTELLIGENCE SUMMARY.

(Erase heading not required.)

Instructions regarding War Diaries and Intelligence Summaries are contained in F. S. Regs., Part II. and the Staff Manual respectively. Title pages will be prepared in manuscript.

September 1917. Serial No. 248.

Place	Date	Hour	Summary of Events and Information	Remarks and references to Appendices
MONCHY CAYEUX 1·9·17			Opened hospital this morning for the reception of sick from Canadian and Secunderabad Brigades and Divisional troops. British sick to be evacuated to No 12 Stationary hospital where they are being treated as local sick and the Indians to be treated in the ambulance until evacuated to Lucknow C.C.S. at Peronne; urgent operations being performed at No 12 Stationary Hosp. One British officer (Capt. Cumming C.A.M.C.) and 4 O.R. attached for duty from Canadian Cav. Fd. Amb.	
			Daily State Morn 1st 9 B.O.R. transfers received from Can C.F.A. 1 B.O. & 4 B.O.R. admitted 1 B.O. & 2 B.O.R. to No 12 Stationary 11 Remaining	
			One riding horse received from railhead yesterday. AMS	
2·9·17			Daily State Morn 2nd 1 B.O. & 20 B.O.R. (including 15 Realies from R.C.D.) admitted 1 B.O. & 18 B.O.R. to No 12 Stationary 13 remaining B.O.R. AMS	

A5834 Wt. W4973/M687 750,000 8/16 D. D. & L. Ltd. Forms/C.2118/13.

Instructions regarding War Diaries and Intelligence Summaries are contained in F. S. Regs., Part II. and the Staff Manual respectively. Title pages will be prepared in manuscript.

WAR DIARY
or
INTELLIGENCE SUMMARY.
(Erase heading not required.)

Army Form C. 2118.

274

Place	Date	Hour	Summary of Events and Information	Remarks and references to Appendices
3.9.17			Capt. C.S.L. Roberts R.A.M.C. rejoined from leave yesterday & proceeded today for duty with to No 5 Convalescent depot today. Representations are being made for his retransfer to this unit owing to his knowledge of Indian troops & an Ind. Cav. Fld. Amb. as he has served here for 1 year & 6 months. 3 O.R. rejoined off leave yesterday & 3 proceeded today. Daily state Noon 3rd 4 B.O.R 1 I.O.R admitted 3 B.O.R to No 12 Stat. 14 B.O.R 12 I.O.R remaining	[illegible]
4.9.17			Capt. D. Ross R.A.M.C. rejoined from temp. duty with R.H.A. Bde yesterday Daily state Noon 4th 9 B.O.R admitted 4 B.O.R. No 12 Stat. 4 B.O.R to duty 15 B.O.R 12 I.O.R remaining	[illegible]
5.9.17			Daily state Noon 5th 10 B.O.R. 1 I.O.R. admitted 5 B.O.R. to No 12 Stat. 20 B.O.R 12 I.O.R. remaining [illegible]	

Instructions regarding War Diaries and Intelligence Summaries are contained in F. S. Regs., Part II. and the Staff Manual respectively. Title pages will be prepared in manuscript.

WAR DIARY
or
INTELLIGENCE SUMMARY.
(Erase heading not required.)

Army Form C. 2118.

275

Place	Date	Hour	Summary of Events and Information	Remarks and references to Appendices
6.9.17			One riding horse evacuated to Mob. Vet. Sec. yesterday.	
			Daily state shown 6th	
			8 B.O.R. admitted 8 B.O.R. to No 12 Stat. 20 B.O.R. 3 I.O.R. remaining 1 I.O.R.	AWS
7.9.17			Daily state shown 7th	
			10 B.O.R. admitted 3 B.O.R. to No 12 Stat. 6 B.O.R. to duty 19 B.O.R. remaining 3 I.O.R.	
8.9.17			The dismounted section & A.D.S. Cars Motors paraded today for inspection by the Military Secretary to the India Office.	AWS
			Daily state shown 8th	
			8 B.O.R. admitted 2 B.O.R. to No 12 Stat. 1 B.O.R. to No 6 Stat. eye case 24 B.O.R. remaining 3 I.O.R.	
9.9.17			Daily state shown 9th	
			4 B.O.R. admitted 3 B.O.R. to No 12 Stat. 1 B.O.R. to No 6 Stat. eye case 24 B.O.R. remaining 3 I.O.R.	AWS
			2 B.O.R. proceeded on leave yesterday	

A5834 Wt. W4973/M687 750,000 8/16 D. D. & L. Ltd. Forms/C.2118/13.

Army Form C. 2118.

276

WAR DIARY
or
INTELLIGENCE SUMMARY.
(*Erase heading not required.*)

Instructions regarding War Diaries and Intelligence Summaries are contained in F. S. Regs., Part II. and the Staff Manual respectively. Title pages will be prepared in manuscript.

Place	Date	Hour	Summary of Events and Information	Remarks and references to Appendices
10.9.17			Daily state noon 10th 3 B.O.R. admitted 3 B.O.R. to No 12 Stat. 6 B.O.R. to duty 18 B.O.R. remaining 1 I.O.R. — 4 I.O.R. — AM	
11.9.17			Daily state noon 11th. 7 B.O.R. / 2 I.O.R. admitted 4 B.O.R. to Lar. Hosp. 4 B.O.R. to duty 17 B.O.R. remaining 6 — AM	
12.9.17			Daily state noon 12th 8 B.O.R. admitted 6 B.O.R. to No 12 Stat. 3 I.O.R. to Lucknow C.C.S. 4 B.O.R. to duty 18 B.O.R. 6 I.O.R. remaining AM	
13.IX.17			Daily state to noon 13th 5 B.O.R. adm. 3 B.O.R. to No 12 Stat. 17 B.O.R. 4 I.O.R. remaining AM	

369

A5834 Wt. W4973/M687 750,000 8/16 D. D. & L. Ltd. Forms/C.2118/13.

Army Form C. 2118.

277

Instructions regarding War Diaries and Intelligence Summaries are contained in F. S. Regs., Part II. and the Staff Manual respectively. Title pages will be prepared in manuscript.

WAR DIARY
or
INTELLIGENCE SUMMARY.
(Erase heading not required.)

Place	Date	Hour	Summary of Events and Information	Remarks and references to Appendices
14.IX.17			To noon 14th 8 B.O.R. adm, 2 B.O.R. to 12 Stat 2 B.O.R. to duty 22 B.O.R. remaining 4 I.O.R. " Lt Col A N FLEMING proceeded on leave on 13th inst date leave from 14-24th Two NCOs & one B.O.R. proceeded on leave. No. T/4/244371 Dr Cowdery A.S.C. adm to hospital this day	
15.IX.17			To noon 15th 11 B.O.R. adm 9 B.O.R. to no 12 Stat and 3 B.O.R. to no 6 Stat 21 B.O.R. remaining I.O.R. adm nil. 2 I.O.R. to Lucknow C.C.S. S.G.J. 2 I.O.R. remaining S.G.J.	
16.IX.17			To noon 16th B.O.R. nil adm 1 B.O.R. to no 12 Stat 4 B.O.R. to duty 16 B.O.R. remaining I.O.R. nil adm I.O.R. 2 remaining Two A.S.C. O.R. rejoined off leave S.G.J.	
17.IX.17			To noon 17th 2 B.O.R. adm 17 B.O.R. remaining 1 I.O.R. adm 3 I.O.R. remaining S.G.J. One NCO rejoined off leave	
18.IX.17			To noon 18th 14 B.O.R. adm 5 B.O.R. to 12 Stat 6 B.O.R. to duty One officer adm One officer to 12 Stat 21 B.O.R. remaining 2 I.O.R. adm 5 I.O.R. remaining S.G.J.	
19.IX.17			To noon 19th 6 B.O.R. adm 1 B.O.R. to 2 Stat 26 B.O.R. remaining 5 I.O.R. remaining	

A5834 Wt. W4973/M687 750,000 8/16 D. D. & L. Ltd. Forms/C.2118/13.

Instructions regarding War Diaries and Intelligence Summaries are contained in F. S. Regs., Part II. and the Staff Manual respectively. Title pages will be prepared in manuscript.

WAR DIARY
or
INTELLIGENCE SUMMARY.
(Erase heading not required.)

Army Form C. 2118.

278

Place	Date	Hour	Summary of Events and Information	Remarks and references to Appendices
19.IX.17 (Cont)			Capt D Ross RAMC proceeded on leave. date of leave 19-29th	
			Two B.O.R. proceeded on leave	
			Capt J. Hunt CAMC joined for temp duty in place of Capt Cummins proceeding on leave on 21.IX.17. S.G.J	
20.IX.17			In hosp 20 / 5 B.O.R. adm / 4 B.O.R. to 12 Stat / 2 B.O.R. to duty / 27 B.O.R. remaining. 59 O.R. remaining	
			One NCO proceeded on French leave for 10 days	
			Two ASC O.R. rejoined off leave	
			Dr Brudenry discharged from hospital.	
			The following joined for duty	
			S.H.R. 446 Hosp Stre Rupn Ass MOHD SARWAR.	
			P.N.A 143 Swp DILWAR	
			AGRA 23 Swp SOOKHA	
			S.H.R. 349 Swp RAMJAN S.G.J	
21.IX.17			In hosp 21 / 10 B.O.R. adm / 12 B.O.R. to 12 Stat / 4 B.O.R. to duty / 22 B.O.R. remaining. One I.O.R. adm / 6 I.O.R. adm	
			No ID 36 Bhisti FAKIR MOHD KHAN adm hospital to-day S.G.J	

A5834 Wt. W4973/M687 750,000 8/16 D. D. & L. Ltd. Forms/C.2118/13.

Army Form C. 2118.

279

Instructions regarding War Diaries and Intelligence Summaries are contained in F. S. Regs., Part II. and the Staff Manual respectively. Title pages will be prepared in manuscript.

WAR DIARY
or
INTELLIGENCE SUMMARY.
(Erase heading not required.)

Place	Date	Hour	Summary of Events and Information	Remarks and references to Appendices
22.IX.17			9 a.m. 22 12 BOR adm 12 BOR to 12 Stat 22 BOR remaining — One IOR adm 7 IOR remaining S.G.J.	
23.IX.17			9 a.m. 23rd 6 BOR adm 5 BOR to 12 Stat 2 BOR to duty 11 BOR remaining — One IOR adm 8 IOR remaining. One NCO & 2 OR proceeded on leave from 24.9.17 – 4-10-17 S.G.J.	
24.IX.17			9 a.m. 24th 6 BOR adm 3 BOR to 12 Stat 1 BOR to duty 20 BOR remaining — one IO adm one IO & 8 OR remaining S.G.J.	
25.IX.17			9 a.m. 25th 9 BOR adm 6 BOR to 12 Stat one BOR to duty 22 BOR remaining 5 IOR to Lucknow C.C.S one IO & 3 OR remaining and one NCO and 2 BOR rejoined from leave. Lt Col A.H. FLEMING I.M.S.	S.G. Johnston Capt RAMC

A5834 Wt. W4973/M687 750,000 8/16 D. D. & L. Ltd. Forms/C.2118/13.

Instructions regarding War Diaries and Intelligence Summaries are contained in F. S. Regs., Part II. and the Staff Manual respectively. Title pages will be prepared in manuscript.

WAR DIARY
or
INTELLIGENCE SUMMARY.
(Erase heading not required.)

Army Form C. 2118.

280

Place	Date	Hour	Summary of Events and Information	Remarks and references to Appendices
26.9.17			Daily state to noon 26th admitted 9 B.O.R. 1 I.O.R. to 12 Stat 9 B.O.R. to duty 2 B.O.R. remaining 14 B.O.R. 1 I.O. 4 I.O.R. D.D.M.S. Cavalry Corps inspected the hospital & camp today. Lt G.S. Ouincup proceeded today for a three days anti gas course at Cavalry Corps H.Q.	
27.9.17			Daily state to noon 27th admitted 9 B.O.R. to 12 Stat. 7 B.O.R. to duty 1 B.O.R. remaining 21 B.O.R. 1 I.O. 4 I.O.R.	
28.9.17			Daily state to noon 28th. admitted 9 B.O.R. to 12 Stat. 4 B.O.R. to duty 2 B.O.R. 1 I.O.R. remaining 24 B.O.R. 1 I.O. 3 I.O.R.	
29.9.17			Daily state to noon 29th admitted 8 B.O.R. 2 I.O.R. to 12 Stat. 6 B.O.R. to duty 2 B.O.R. 1 I.O.R. remaining 24 B.O.R. 1 I.O. 4 I.O.R.	
30.9.17			Daily state to noon 30th admitted 4 B.O.R. to 12 Stat. 6 B.O.R. to duty 4 B.O.R. remaining 18 B.O.R. 1 I.O. 4 I.O.R. Capt. D. Ross R.A.M.C. & 2 O.Ranks returned from leave. Lt Ouincup returned from anti gas course. One O.R. proceeded on leave yesterday. S Aldridge A. No T3/024496 evacuated to No 12 Stat. with PUO measles. A. L. Fleming Lt. Col.	

6ck. 19/7

S/

Secunderabad Cav. F. A.

Medical | See bad | 1 C.F.A.

Instructions regarding War Diaries and Intelligence Summaries are contained in F. S. Regs., Part II. and the Staff Manual respectively. Title pages will be prepared in manuscript.

WAR DIARY
or
INTELLIGENCE SUMMARY.
(Erase heading not required.)

Army Form C. 2118.

~~271~~ 248

Place	Date	Hour	Summary of Events and Information	Remarks and references to Appendices
MONCHY CAYEUX	1.10.17		Daily state [illegible] 1st	
			8 B.O.R. admitted 7 B.O.R. to No 12 Stn. 2 B.O.R. to duty 17 B.O.R. 1 O.O. 4 O.R. remaining.	
			Capt. Ross & 2 other ranks returned from leave yesterday.	
			[illegible] evacuated sick yesterday.	
	2.10.17		Daily state [illegible] 2nd admitted 7 B.O.R. 2 O.R. to No 12 Stn. 8 B.O.R. to duty 4 B.O.R. remaining 12 B.O.R. 1 O.O. 5 O.R.	
			[illegible] O.R. returned from leave yesterday.	
	3.10.17		Daily state [illegible] 3rd admitted 7 B.O.R. to No 12 Stn. 2 B.O.R. remaining 17 B.O.R. 1 O.O. 2 O.R.	
			Capt. Johnson R.A.M.C. & Capt. Hunt R.A.M.C. [illegible]	
			Cav. Corps H.Q.	
	4.10.17		Daily state [illegible] 4th	
			admitted 4 B.O.R. (1 French Civilian) to duty 3 B.O.R. remaining 1 O.O. 18 B.O.R. 6 O.R.	
			Rev. Cannonwood proceeded on leave to England today.	

A5834 Wt. W4973/M687 750,000 8/16 D. D. & L. Ltd. Forms/C.2118/13.

Instructions regarding War Diaries and Intelligence Summaries are contained in F. S. Regs., Part II. and the Staff Manual respectively. Title pages will be prepared in manuscript.

WAR DIARY
or
INTELLIGENCE SUMMARY.
(Erase heading not required.)

Army Form C. 2118.

282

Place	Date	Hour	Summary of Events and Information	Remarks and references to Appendices
5.10.17			Daily state to noon 5th Admitted 10 B.O.R. Dis to 12 Stat. 5 B.O.R. to Lechine C.S. 1 ?.O.R. remaining 19 O.R. 23 B.O.R. 5? O.R. Orders received at noon today to march North tomorrow. Packing up & clearing during the afternoon. [illegible]	
6.10.17 ST MARTIN			Daily state to noon 6th admitted 10 B.O.R. 3 ? O.R. Dis to 12 Stat 41 B.O.R. to Lechine C.C.S. 1 ?.O. 5 ?.O.R. [illegible] 3 ? 3 ? O.R. to duty 2 B.O.R. Nil remaining. Marched at 9.15 to ST MARTIN near AIRE about 20 miles a very wet day	
7.10.17 WATOU			Marched to Watou about 23 miles another wet day. Did not reach billets (a field) till dark. Daily state to noon 7th 2 B.O.R. admitted & transferred to 12 Stat.	
8.10.17			Halted today. Daily state to noon 8th 2 B.O.R. admitted & transferred to 2 C.C.S. 1 B.O.R. — — 3 C.C.S. Fine morning, wet afternoon. The personnel have got into tents in another camping ground. [illegible]	

A5834 Wt. W4973/M687 750,000 8/16 D. D. & L. Ltd. Forms/C.2118/13.

Instructions regarding War Diaries and Intelligence Summaries are contained in F. S. Regs., Part II. and the Staff Manual respectively. Title pages will be prepared in manuscript.

WAR DIARY
or
INTELLIGENCE SUMMARY.
(Erase heading not required.)

Army Form C. 2118.

283

Place	Date	Hour	Summary of Events and Information	Remarks and references to Appendices
	14.10.17		Have halted at WATOU all week. The weather has been very bad, raining every day until today when it has cleared up. The ambulance has been situated in a field where the mud has got very bad. Tents & trench covers have been issued and the men have all got under cover. The animals are all in the open. For several days part of the personnel and the officers were billeted in a farm near by where cover for riding horses was obtained but this had to be evacuated on arrival of Cambrian Bde.	
			The motor cycle belonging to Motor Cyclist Turner was stolen on 10th in POPERINGHE while he was doing duty with A.D.M.S. A court of enquiry was held.	
			A medical board to report on fitness for a permanent commission of Lt. Murray. [illegible] was held this morning	
			Orders received today to march westwards tomorrow to RENESCURE near ST OMER.	
			Daily state.	
			8th to 9th 1 O.R. admitted 2 B.O.R. 1 O.R. to C.C.S.	
			9th to 10th 1 officer 1 B.O.R. 1 O.R. admitted & transferred C.C.S. The officer belonged to R.F.C. and had an accident his machine falling in the vicinity of the camp.	
			10–11th 2 B.O.R. 1 O.R. admitted & transferred. 11th to 12th nil. 12th to 13th 3 B.O.R. 2 O.R. admitted and transferred 13th to 14th 2 B.O.R. admitted & transferred	
			AM	

A5834 Wt. W4973/M687 750,000 8/16 D. D. & L. Ltd. Forms/C.2118/13.

Instructions regarding War Diaries and Intelligence Summaries are contained in F. S. Regs., Part II. and the Staff Manual respectively. Title pages will be prepared in manuscript.

WAR DIARY
or
INTELLIGENCE SUMMARY.
(Erase heading not required.)

Army Form C. 2118.

284

Place	Date	Hour	Summary of Events and Information	Remarks and references to Appendices
BAURINGHEM	15.10.17		Marched to BAURINGHEM about 25 miles a fine & sunny day reached camp before dark. Billeted in a village.	
			Daily state [illegible] 15 6 O.R. admitted [illegible] transferred	
			While in POPERINGHE area sick have been evacuated to REMY siding arrangements had been made there by sending a party from [illegible] until [illegible] were evacuated to OUSTERLINE where there is a detachment of the [illegible] the Remount depots.	
WILLAMETZ	16.10.17		Marched to FAUQUEMBERGUES about 19 miles a fine day [illegible]	[illegible]
FRUGES	17.10.17		Marched to FRUGES 10 kilometres & went into permanent billets. [illegible]	[illegible]
	22.10.17		Some difficulty has been experienced in getting all horses under cover. [illegible] has been opened. At present a camp in the town but now an excellent building the clinique [illegible] of the local hospice has been taken over which makes an excellent hospital.	[illegible]

Instructions regarding War Diaries and Intelligence Summaries are contained in F. S. Regs., Part II. and the Staff Manual respectively. Title pages will be prepared in manuscript.

WAR DIARY
or
INTELLIGENCE SUMMARY.
(*Erase heading not required.*)

Army Form C. 2118.

2

Place	Date	Hour	Summary of Events and Information	Remarks and references to Appendices
22.10.17 contd			Lt. Oswincef has been placed in charge of troops quartered in [illegible] and Capt. Ross in charge of the hospital.	
			Lt Bannerjee departed on 15th for duty with Lahore 2nd Gen Hosp at Alexandria	
			Ptes Burtonwood & Brigant transferred to No 15 C.C.S. on 16th	
			Cpl Green proceeded on leave on 17th & Lt. Sampson 22nd	
			A Pioneer Battalion was despatched on 19th. Pte Lewis R.A.M.C. ~~[illegible]~~ with the medical party under Capt. Bergmann was supplied with Med. equipment from this unit. [illegible] who also was [illegible]	
			Pte J. Conlan R.A.M.C. transferred to this unit on 20th from W. Battery	
			" G. Scotcher "	
			Pte J. W. Baillie	
			But the last named has not yet joined & Pte J. Scotcher is on leave	
			A.M.L.	

A5834 Wt. W4973/M687 750,000 8/16 D. D. & L. Ltd. Forms/C.2118/13.

Instructions regarding War Diaries and Intelligence Summaries are contained in F. S. Regs., Part II. and the Staff Manual respectively. Title pages will be prepared in manuscript.

WAR DIARY
or
INTELLIGENCE SUMMARY.
(Erase heading not required.)

Army Form C. 2118.

288

Place	Date	Hour	Summary of Events and Information	Remarks and references to Appendices
	31.10.17		The ambulance has remained billetted in FRUGES. The fresh mounted section paraded last week under Capt. L. C. Johnston R.A.M.C. One British O.R. proceeded on leave on 28th. Men and animals are all comfortably under shelter now. G.O.C. Sec. Bde visited the hospital on 27th.	
			Daily state	
			To noon 23rd 3 B.O.R. 1 I.O.R. admitted 1 I.O.R. to duty 12 B.O.R. 6 I.O.R. remaining.	
			24th 4 B.O.R 2 I.O.R " 3 B.O.R. to C.C.S 2 B.O.R. to duty 11 B.O.R. 8 I.O.R remaining	
			25th 3 B.O.R. " 1 I.O.R. to [illegible] Stat. Hosp. 14 B.O.R. 7 I.O.R. remaining	
			26th 1 B.O.R. " 1 B.O.R. to C.C.S 1 B.O.R. to duty 13 B.O.R. 7 I.O.R. remaining	
			27th 4 B.O.R 1 I.O.R. " 2 B.O.R to C.C.S. 3 B.O.R. 1 I.O.R. to duty 12 B.O.R. 7 I.O.R. remaining	
			28th 2 B.O.R 7 I.O.R (4 sweepers?) " 2 B.O.R to C.C.S 12 B.O.R 14 I.O.R remaining	
			29th 2 B.O.R. 1 I.O.R. " 2 B.O.R to C.C.S 1 B.O.R 4 I.O.R. to duty 11 B.O.R. 11 I.O.R. remaining	
			30th 3 B.O.R. 2 I.O.R. " 2 B.O.R. to C.C.S 2 B.O.R. to duty 10 B.O.R. 13 I.O.R. remaining	
			31st 4 B.O.R. 2 I.O.R. (sweepers?) (sweepers?) " 2 B.O.R 2 I.O.R. to C.C.S 2 B.O.R. 2 I.O.R. to duty 12 B.O.R. 11 I.O.R. remaining	
			The two Indians evacuated yesterday to I Stat. at FREVENT were not taken in there but were sent on to PERONNE.	
			One N.C.O. & 5 sweepers from Sanitary Sect. reported for duty in Fruges on 27th.	
			A. L. Fleming Lt. Col. IMS	

A5834 Wt. W4973/M687 750,000 8/16 D. D. & L. Ltd. Forms/C.2118/13.

Nov. 1917

Secunderabad Cav. F.A.

Instructions regarding War Diaries and Intelligence Summaries are contained in F. S. Regs., Part II. and the Staff Manual respectively. Title pages will be prepared in manuscript.

WAR DIARY
or
INTELLIGENCE SUMMARY.
(Erase heading not required.)

286

Army Form C. 2118.

248

Place	Date	Hour	Summary of Events and Information	Remarks and references to Appendices
8.11.17 Frugès			a Divisional route march was held on 3rd & marched past G.O.C. Division	
			Capt. J.C. Johnston Lt. [illegible] proceeded on leave for 14 days to Paris on 6th & 7th respectively	
			The following have joined the unit	
			Dr. Beasley H. A.S.C. T4/059489	
			- Gotts T.W. - T4/059479	
			- Mitchell J. - T4/253474	
			Cowderay W. - T4/244371	
			One horsed ambulance wagon attached to 7th [illegible] temporarily from 4th till today	
			Orders received yesterday to march on 9th. Hospital is being closed today & all patients evacuated & preparations for march at 8 a.m. tomorrow morning	
10.11.17 DOMONTIGNY			Marched at 8 a.m. yesterday via HESDIN to LE QUESNEL FARM a few kilometres west of DOULLENS a distance of 33 miles. after dark owing to directions given by a Frenchman the transport took a turning marked on the map a second class road this was found to be no road at all & the carts got stuck.	

A5834 Wt. W4973/M687 750,000 8/16 D. D. & L. Ltd. Forms/C.2118/13.

Instructions regarding War Diaries and Intelligence Summaries are contained in F. S. Regs., Part II. and the Staff Manual respectively. Title pages will be prepared in manuscript.

WAR DIARY
or
INTELLIGENCE SUMMARY.
(Erase heading not required.)

287

Army Form C. 2118.

Place	Date	Hour	Summary of Events and Information	Remarks and references to Appendices
10.11.17 Contd			The mules being tired refused to pull when turning them on a field and the carts had to be unloaded & man handled round; by this time it was nearly 12 o'clock and the mules would not pull when the carts were on the road, so the carts were left & the mules brought to camp about 6 kilometres off. Got in at 2 a.m. The ambulances owing to late start & tyre trouble en route did not get in till midnight. Men had no kits & little food this night, owing to carts not getting in. At 6.30 a.m. the mules were sent back for the carts & got them out. Marched at 9 a.m. but the tired mules stuck on a heavy hill at the start. Part of the transport got in about 6 p.m. the rest had stuck about 6 kilometres short at RUBEMPRE. Ambulances got in about 6.30 p.m.	[illegible]
11-11-17 MORCOURT			Did not march till 4 p.m. to MORCOURT. The rest of the transport joined up on in the morning & the night march was uneventful reaching billets about 9 p.m.	[illegible]
12.11.17 ESTREES LA CHAUSSEE			Marched about 4 p.m. & reached billets about 10 p.m. During the day Pte J. SANSON A.S.C. had his hand badly damaged by a detonator exploding in a fire when he was stooping down to dry his gloves. A number of these were found lying about the billets.	[illegible]

A5834 Wt. W4973/M687 750,000 8/16 D. D. & L. Ltd. Forms/C.2118/13.

Instructions regarding War Diaries and Intelligence Summaries are contained in F. S. Regs., Part II. and the Staff Manual respectively. Title pages will be prepared in manuscript.

WAR DIARY
or
INTELLIGENCE SUMMARY.
(Erase heading not required.)

288

Army Form C. 2118.

Place	Date	Hour	Summary of Events and Information	Remarks and references to Appendices
13-11-17			Cpl. A. WINGROVE A.S.C. M1/08147 who was [illegible] with [illegible] on 9th died in hospital on 10-11-17. No 8.358 Pte J. BAILEY [illegible] appointed a/Cpl from 20-10-17 Marched this afternoon to ROISEL. The place is crowded with troops [illegible] a road, and only cellars & a few poor shelters for the men. 7 [illegible] by [illegible] Commandant	
15-11-17			Getting more comfortably settled. Most of the men have made themselves pretty comfortable under in cellars, about 13 horses in stables & getting others in standings [illegible] buildings without roofs	[illegible]
18-11-17			Orders have been received that the [illegible] expected [illegible]. The Pack [illegible] will be [illegible] move. Attended a conference of [illegible] of the Brigade today when the scheme was explained. The role of this Division is to pass through the Infantry when they in conjunction with the tanks have captured the enemy's trench system.	[illegible]

A5834 Wt. W4973/M687 750,000 8/16 D. D. & L. Ltd. Forms/C.2118/13.

Instructions regarding War Diaries and Intelligence Summaries are contained in F. S. Regs., Part II. and the Staff Manual respectively. Title pages will be prepared in manuscript.

WAR DIARY
or
INTELLIGENCE SUMMARY.
(Erase heading not required.)

289

Army Form C. 2118.

Place	Date	Hour	Summary of Events and Information	Remarks and references to Appendices
18.11.17	Contd		The Secunderabad Brigade is intended to cross the St Quentin canal at the locks at MARCOING [illegible] the Canadian Cav. Bde. which is the advance unit, will be pushed forward as far as possible [illegible] CAMBRAI from the east [illegible] there to seize the crossings on the SENSEE river and hold them (i.e. the North & N.E. of CAMBRAI). The 2nd Cav. Div. follows the [illegible] & the infantry will be pushed up as quickly as possible. Medical arrangements. Each Mounted section [illegible] with Brigades. C.C. Field Ambulance will be attached to Bde. H.Q. A.D.S. will remain behind until ordered. [illegible] will be pushed up to divisional report centre as soon as possible. Motor ambulances with a party of stretcher bearers will move forward as soon after the Cavalry as possible & wait at forward report centre [illegible] as the situation [illegible]. A C.M.S. will establish an A.D.S. at [illegible] across the Escaut Canal as soon as possible. Tent sections of field ambulances will remain behind and not be used. A Echelon is to be divided into 2 portions A 1 & A 2. The C.D.S. will [illegible] A 2 Echelon. S. Henry J. P. No 27458 A.S.C. Bearer Narasimuloo V A.B.C. No 9207 " Latchman IV No 9238 Sweeper MARIDAS No 205/421 9579 A.H.C. } Evacuated sick The motor ambulances attached with Cavalry Corps H.Q. rejoined on 17.11.17. [illegible initials]	

A5834 Wt. W4973/M687 750,000 8/16 D. D. & L. Ltd. Forms/C.2118/13.

Army Form C. 2118.

290

Instructions regarding War Diaries and Intelligence Summaries are contained in F. S. Regs., Part II. and the Staff Manual respectively. Title pages will be prepared in manuscript.

WAR DIARY
or
INTELLIGENCE SUMMARY.
(Erase heading not required.)

Place	Date	Hour	Summary of Events and Information	Remarks and references to Appendices
24.11.17 CHUIGNOLLES			On 19th it was announced that Z day was 20th & zero hour 6.20 a.m. The B.M.S. marched with the Brigade at 1 a.m. on 20th to BOIS DESSART close to FINS reaching that place about zero hour. Z A echelon with the whole ambulance except [illegible] wagons [illegible] by formation of B.M.S. (which remained at [illegible]SE [illegible]) brought along next day by [illegible] [illegible] (from B echelon) marched about 2.30 a.m. On arrival at B. DESSART horses were watered & fed and the men had a bit [illegible]. At 8.45 all were saddled up & the [illegible] ready to march off on [illegible] orders. Reports from the front were very favourable but the [illegible] advance did not come till about midday. The Brigade moved at a trot to VILLERS PLOUICH & [illegible] up to MARCOING where it was found that Canadian Bde was held up at MASNIERES the bridge having been broken by a tank & the right of the Infantry attack having been held up. The Brigade formed up [illegible] the village and patrol squadrons were sent forward. In one of the squadrons of 7th D.Gs a good many casualties occurred & they were handed over to the Infantry medical services. The Brigade remained at this place without moving till after dark. Some Infantry casualties (10) were found in a German dug out and one man of B.M.G. Squadron (slightly wounded leg & head) was placed with them & [illegible] to as far as possible & information sent to [illegible] to arrange their evacuation. Marched back [illegible] about a mile & bivouacked for the night. Next day stood to all day & moved back [illegible] next evening to the spot where the [illegible] [illegible] A echelon were parked. Next morning (21st) the Brigade marched back by a [illegible] via the MARCOING [illegible] & FINS [illegible] [illegible] p.m. and in the evening [illegible] of [illegible] B.M.S. [illegible] next of the Ambulance with A2 echelon at EQUANCOURT. [illegible]	(about 100)

A5834 Wt. W4973/M687 750,000 8/16 D. D. & L. Ltd. Forms/C.2118/13.

291

Army Form C. 2118.

Instructions regarding War Diaries and Intelligence Summaries are contained in F. S. Regs., Part II. and the Staff Manual respectively. Title pages will be prepared in manuscript.

WAR DIARY
or
INTELLIGENCE SUMMARY.

(Erase heading not required.)

Place	Date	Hour	Summary of Events and Information	Remarks and references to Appendices
24.11.17 contd			On 23rd the Ambulance marched in rear of the Brigade to CHUIGNOLLES. Owing to the wavy road being blocked at CAPPY and watering en route we did not reach destination till after dark. Good cover for animals and all ranks under roofs.	
			I interviewed the A.D.M.S. today suggesting that in the event of limbered wagons proceeding with the Bde a light A.D.S. should go with it, instead of the Cash Mounted Section, the Cavalry with the C.M.S. Being unlikely to put extra animals in the vehicles. The A.D.M.S. asked me to interview the Brigadier on the matter, which I did. He approved of my scheme and a light A.D.S. has been organised consisting of 3 limbered wagons with 6 mules each, 3 horsed ambulances with 4 each, 2 M.O.s mounted with mounted grooms, a motor cyclist, and 7 personnel in each horsed ambulance.	
30.11.17			On 27th the ambulance marched to TREFCON with the Bde and went into huts & stables there already prepared by the R.E. Cover for all men & animals. ~~We are~~ The division was expected to take over the line it had held in the summer and the A.D.M.S. had settled that this ambulance was to take over the M.D.S. at BERNES again. The relief was to take place during the night of 1/2nd. But this morning sudden orders arrived that the division was to move at once mounted. And from what we heard this was necessitated by a surprise attack of the Germans driving back our line & hasty reinforcements being required	

A5834 Wt. W4973/M687 750,000 8/16 D. D. & L. Ltd. Forms/C.2118/13.

WAR DIARY
or
INTELLIGENCE SUMMARY.
(Erase heading not required.)

202

Army Form C. 2118.

Instructions regarding War Diaries and Intelligence Summaries are contained in F. S. Regs., Part II. and the Staff Manual respectively. Title pages will be prepared in manuscript.

Place	Date	Hour	Summary of Events and Information	Remarks and references to Appendices
30.11.17 cont^d			The Ambulance marched behind the Bde to VILLERS FAUCON. Owing to frequent halts from traffic on the roads, destination was not reached till about 6 p.m. and the Ambulance was parked in a field. The Staff Capt. left a message saying the Bde had gone forward and that the Ambulance was not required as the Infantry was making all medical arrangements. Lieut. [illegible] RAMC with 20 [illegible] attached to M.D.S. VILLERS FAUCON but [illegible] were withdrawn	
			Daily states for the month	
	1st	9 noon	Admissions 7 B.O.R. 1 I.O.R. remaining 19 B.O.R. 12 I.O.R.	
	2nd	–	7 – nil to C.C.S. 6 B.O.R. to duty 2 B.O.R. remaining 19 B.O.R. 12 I.O.R.	
	3rd	–	1 B.O. 6 B.O.R. 1 I.O.R. to C.C.S. 1 B.O. 2 B.O.R. remaining 11 B.O.R. 13 I.O.R.	
	4th	–	7 B.O.R. to C.C.S. 6 – duty 2 B.O.R. remaining 11 B.O.R. 13 I.O.R.	
	5th	–	7 B.O.R. – 6 B.O.R. duty remaining 11 B.O.R. 13 I.O.R.	
	6th	–	3 B.O.R. – 5 B.O.R. duty 2 B.O.R. remaining 18 B.O.R. 8 I.O.R.	
	7th	–	4 B.O.R. – 6 B.O.R. 5 I.O.R. remaining 16 B.O.R. 8 I.O.R.	
	8th	–	5 – – 1 B.O.R. duty 2 B.O.R. 5 I.O.R. remaining 13 B.O.R. 3 I.O.R.	
	9th	–	10 B.O.R. 1 I.O. 2 I.O.R. to C.C.S. 28 B.O.R. 1 I.O. 5 I.O.R. remaining nil	
	10th	–	4 B.O.R. 1 I.O.R. C.C.S. 4 B.O.R. 1 I.O.R. nil remaining	
	11th	nil		
	12th		1 B.O.R. admitted & transferred 1 I.O.R. admitted & remaining	

A5834 Wt. W4973/M687 750,000 8/16 D. D. & L. Ltd. Forms/C.2118/13.

Instructions regarding War Diaries and Intelligence Summaries are contained in F. S. Regs., Part II. and the Staff Manual respectively. Title pages will be prepared in manuscript.

WAR DIARY
or
INTELLIGENCE SUMMARY.
(*Erase heading not required.*)

293

Army Form C. 2118.

Place	Date	Hour	Summary of Events and Information	Remarks and references to Appendices
	January 13th		Admitted 2 B.O.R 1 I.O.R. to C.C.S. 2 B.O.R. 2 I.O.R.	
	— 14th		— 5 B.O.R. C.C.S 5 B.O.R nil remaining	
	— 15th		— 1 B.O. 2 B.O.R. 2 I.O.R. evacuated	
	— 16th		— 2 B.O.R. 2 I.O.R. evacuated	
	— 17th		— 4 B.O.R. 2 I.O.R —	
	— 18th		— 5 B.O.R. 1 I.O.R — (2 [illegible])	
	— 19th		— 1 B.O.R. 2 I.O.R — (1 B.O.R. [illegible])	
	— 20th		— 4 B.O.R. 4 I.O.R. (1 B.O.R. [illegible])	
	21st 22nd 23rd		} nil.	
	— 24th		— 8 I.O.R evacuated	
	— 25th		— 2 B.O.R. 1 I.O.R. evacuated	
	— 26th		— 6 B.O.R 4 I.O.R —	
	— 27th		— 4 — 1 —	
	— 28		4 — 1 — — (4 B.O.R. [illegible])	
	— 29		3 — — (2 B.O.R [illegible])	
	— 30		2 — 0 I.O.R. — (1 B.O.R [illegible])	

[illegible]

A5834 Wt. W4973/M687 750,000 8/16 D. D. & L. Ltd. Forms/C.2118/13.

Dec. 1917

Secunderabad F. A.

Medical

Instructions regarding War Diaries and Intelligence Summaries are contained in F. S. Regs., Part II. and the Staff Manual respectively. Title pages will be prepared in manuscript.

WAR DIARY
or
INTELLIGENCE SUMMARY.
(Erase heading not required.)

December 1917

Secbad [illegible]

~~244~~

Army Form C. 2118.

248.

Place	Date	Hour	Summary of Events and Information	Remarks and references to Appendices
			Map reference 1-40000 [illegible] organisation map sheet 2	
Between VILLERS FAUCON & LIERAMONT	7.12.17		Early on the morning of 1st (about 2 A.M.) I received a message from A.D.M.S. to report myself to him. I reported to him at advanced report centre of Division at W 29 d 9.0. and he directed me to report to Bde H.Q. which I found at W29 C 8 3 reaching there about 5 a.m. The whole Brigade were located in this vicinity standing to. On my recommendation the A.D.S. was ordered up to HEUDECOURT which they reached about midday & prepared to open at W21 a 3 5. The Brigade stood to all day. Lt. G.S. [illegible] O.R.C. U.S.A. doing temporary duty with Poona Horse was evacuated sick this day suffering from [illegible] and Lt. [illegible] I.M.S. placed in temp. med. ch. of Poona Horse. Sub [illegible] Terry was ~~left at~~ put in charge of Tent Sect. of Ambulance left at VILLERS FAUCON (no officer being available). In the evening orders were received for the Brigade to take over the line held by Ambala Bde. The relief taking place that night. The A.D.S. opened in HEUDECOURT and an advanced post established consisting of all available bearers under Capt. [illegible] at REVELON FARM W 16 10, 7. Touch was established with the R.A.P.s that night situated at W 6 d 3 7 X 1 C 25 7 X 1 C 10 2. Bde H.Q. moved to W 16 a 7, 8. On 2nd I visited R.A.P.s and found it was a very long carry for the bearers. Arranged that wheeled carriers would run along HEUDECOURT GOUZEAUCOURT road and so save some carrying. Also an Infantry field ambulance open at HEUDECOURT lent some bearers (4 squads) to be at REVELON farm & help our men. In the evening the line was handed over to a battalion formed from 1st Division. Relief completed about midnight. During the day about 60 casualties had been dealt with, the majority from other formations including some German prisoners. On 3rd the Bde moved back to the present position [illegible] has been ready [illegible] the time at [illegible] notice during day & 1 hours during night. 1 S.A.S. [illegible] has been attached to M. corps dressing station FINS to assist with Indian sick [illegible]. A [illegible] battalion is ready [illegible] off with it will proceed a party from the Ambulance consisting of 2 N.C.O.s, 3 [illegible] of Ambulance, 24 stretcher bearers 2 W. orderlies 2 cooks & 2 [illegible]. The weather has been very cold with hard frost, but today is milder. Health of the Brigade throughout has been excellent.	

A5834 Wt. W4973/M687 750,000 8/16 D. D. & L. Ltd. Forms/C.2118/13.

Instructions regarding War Diaries and Intelligence Summaries are contained in F. S. Regs., Part II. and the Staff Manual respectively. Title pages will be prepared in manuscript.

WAR DIARY
or
INTELLIGENCE SUMMARY.
(Erase heading not required.)

Army Form C. 2118.

295

Place	Date	Hour	Summary of Events and Information	Remarks and references to Appendices
16.12.17			On 8th the Bde moved back to BUIRE. Did not reach camp till after dark owing to congestion of traffic on the road. Camped in a muddy field, horses being under incomplete shelter & personnel in 4 French huts. Rations did not turn up nor were rugs carried on Bde H Q wagon. The Bde H Q & two regiments had to change their bivouac at the last minute owing to COURCELLES being infected with horse disease. On 9th the scheme came into operation & rations are being drawn by horse transport. Permission was obtained to move the medical personnel & equipment to COURCELLES leaving wagon lines in the same place. Move completed by evening & preparations made to open hospital. An encampment of 13 Nissen huts & one Adrian was taken, where a hospital could be opened if necessary for the Division. This morning have been informed that this encampment cannot be held so we are moving to a smaller encampment adjoining. I proceed this afternoon to act as A.D.M.S. 5th Cav. Div. and hand over command of the unit to Capt. L. C. Johnston R.A.M.C. during the absence of Col. Macnab D.S.O. on one months leave. A. L. Fleming Lt. Col. RAMC	

A5834 Wt. W4973/M687 750,000 8/16 D. D. & L. Ltd. Forms/C.2118/13.

Instructions regarding War Diaries and Intelligence Summaries are contained in F. S. Regs., Part II. and the Staff Manual respectively. Title pages will be prepared in manuscript.

WAR DIARY
or
INTELLIGENCE SUMMARY.
(Erase heading not required.)

Army Form C. 2118.

296

Place	Date	Hour	Summary of Events and Information	Remarks and references to Appendices
11 XII 17			4 [illegible] Adm 4 Br remaining Indians nil [illegible]	
12 XII 17			4 Br Adm 5 Br remaining Indians 4 sick adm 4 Indians remaining [illegible]	
13 XII 17			5 Br Adm 5 Br Evacuated CCS one Br to [illegible] [illegible] Br remaining Indians one adm 3 evacuated to CCS 2 remaining Dr Aldridge rejoined from [illegible] on completion of 14 days [illegible]	[illegible]
14 XII 17			Lieut [illegible] NORMAN evacuated sick to 55 CCS [illegible] The wagon lines joined up with the rest of the 4th Amb this day. Capt [illegible] COLLINS [illegible] joined for temporary duty yesterday 1 Br Off & 2 Br OR Adm, One Off evacuated to CCS Remaining 9 Indians One Off adm & 9 OR to CCS One Off & 6 OR Remaining 5 [illegible]	
15 XII 17			2 Br adm & 2 evacuated to CCS [illegible] Remaining Six Indian Off adm & 5 OR One Off & 5 OR evacuated 5 Remaining Orders received today from ADMS [illegible] G.S.O [illegible] to be struck off strength from 14 XII 17 [illegible]	
16 XII 17			5 Br adm 4 Evacuated 2 [illegible] 3 to duty 5 remaining 4 Indian adm 4 Evacuated 5 remaining	[illegible]
17 XII 17			5 Br adm 2 Evacuated 2 [illegible] 5 transferred to [illegible] I to duty nil remaining 3 Indians adm 4 evacuated 5 transferred to [illegible] to duty nil remaining The 4th Amb marched this day to TREFCON [illegible] Kitchen [illegible] proceeded this day to India & struck off strength [illegible] DAVIS [illegible]	
18 XII 17			1 Br Off adm 3 OR adm and transferred to [illegible] 3 Indian adm & transferred to [illegible]	[illegible]

A5834 Wt. W4973/M687 750,000 8/16 D. D. & L. Ltd. Forms/C.2118/13.

Army Form C. 2118.

WAR DIARY
or
INTELLIGENCE SUMMARY.

(*Erase heading not required.*)

Instructions regarding War Diaries and Intelligence Summaries are contained in F. S. Regs., Part II. and the Staff Manual respectively. Title pages will be prepared in manuscript.

297

Place	Date	Hour	Summary of Events and Information	Remarks and references to Appendices
19 XII 17			Information received from O/C Workshops that No M S 3181 Pte G E SHELDON ASC MT evacuated to 41 Stationary hospital on 17 XII 17. Admitted to hospital Drs ~~Baker~~ ~~Brown~~ T29722 BAKER T29210 BROWN T4/059479 GOTTS T4/253474 NUTTALL to-day. Two N C Os allotted new number 5714 Sgt DAVIES FJ new number H/45668 6850 A/Cpl TYNET new number H/45646 [illegible]	
20 XII 17			9 Br adm 4 evacuated 5 remaining One Indian adm sent to CCS	
			No 42653 Pte LUNBT RAYNE proceeded temp duty with supply column 5th Cav Div. [illegible]	
21 XII 17			No 1243 Dr NARASIMULU ABC adm & evacuated to CCS on 20 XII 17. No 9237 1st grade servant VALANGANNY adm hospital to day. No 9231 NARASIMULU ABC adm hospital. No 9179 Dr MYSANNAH ABC adm & evacuated to CCS for N Y D Mental. 3 Br adm 5 remaining 4 Indians adm one evacuated 3 remaining [illegible]	
22 XII 17			No M2/032933 Pte TURNER ASC MT proceeded this day for temp duty with D D M S Cav Corps	
			17 Br adm 14 evacuated 3 Sabres st 5 remaining One Indian adm 1 evacuated 3 remaining [illegible]	
23 XII 17			No T/213232 Dr EDWARDS R adm hospital and transferred to Corps rest st along with Dr GOTTS & BROWN J W. No 9227 Dr DOSANNAH ABC adm hospital No 9206 Dr PENTIANNAH ABC adm & transferred to CCS 7 Br adm 5 transferred from 4th Ind Cav FA 7 evacuated 5 to duty 5 remaining 2 Indians adm 1 transferred from 4th Ind Cav FA 6 to CCS 7 Remaining [illegible]	
24 XII 17			No 9237 1st Grade servant VELANGANNY ABC discharged hospital. No T/29722 Dr BAKER F ASC discharged hospital 6 Br adm 3 evacuated 5 to Corps rest Station 5 to Sabres st 3 remaining 3 Indians adm 2 to CCS 4 Remaining [illegible]	

A5834 Wt. W4973/M687 750,000 8/16 D. D. & L. Ltd. Forms/C.2118/13.

Army Form C. 2118.

Instructions regarding War Diaries and Intelligence Summaries are contained in F. S. Regs., Part II. and the Staff Manual respectively. Title pages will be prepared in manuscript.

WAR DIARY
or
INTELLIGENCE SUMMARY.
(Erase heading not required.)

258

Place	Date	Hour	Summary of Events and Information	Remarks and references to Appendices
25 XII 17			7 Br. adm. I.L. C.C.S. 3 to Corps rest St. [illegible] to Duty 7 remaining	
			10 Indians adm. I.L. C.C.S. III to duty 9 remaining. St. Johnston Capt RAMC	
26 XII 17			Capt L C Johnston RAMC on leave to U.K. period 27-12-17 to 10-1-18.	
			#9206 1st grade Cook David A H Corps admitted hosp. yesterday	
			#9189 Bearer Nysammah ABC rejoined from Lucknow C.C.S.	
			Admitted – 1 Br. O.R. Discharged duty – 1. Remaining – 7.	
			4 Ind. O.R. — 4 — 9.	
			Capt. F R Hammond RAMC took over command of unit.	
27-XII-17			9189 Bearer Nysammah / 9205 Bearer Sayannah I } admitted & evacuated to Lucknow C.C.S	
			9227 " Rosannah III / 9206 1st gd. Cook David } evacuated Lucknow C.C.S.	
			9226 L. Naick Sibdyal admitted hospital.	
			Admitted. Br. O.R. – 7. Evacuated C.C.S – 4. Evac. Sec. Hosp. [illegible] 1. Rem. 9	
			" I.O.R. – 3 " 7 " 5	
28 XII 17			Drivers Brown & Edwards ASC rejoined from C.C.R. Station.	
			9236 – Bearer Latchman IV / 52 Water Carrier Ramasawmy } admitted hospital	
			Admitted B.O.R. – 1, Evac C.C.S 1. Trans C.R.Sta 3. Rem. 6.	
			I.O.R. – 4 2 from #7 CFA " 8.	

A5834 Wt. W4973/M687 750,000 8/16 D. D. & L. Ltd. Forms/C.2118/13.

Instructions regarding War Diaries and Intelligence Summaries are contained in F. S. Regs., Part II. and the Staff Manual respectively. Title pages will be prepared in manuscript.

WAR DIARY
or
INTELLIGENCE SUMMARY.
(Erase heading not required.)

Army Form C. 2118.

299

Place	Date	Hour	Summary of Events and Information	Remarks and references to Appendices
29-XII-17			Wate Carrier Ramasawmy – discharged to duty.	
			#9231 Bear Narasimulu VII evac. C.C.S. (Lucknow)	
			Admitted. Br. Off 1. C.C.S. – Off 1. Rem	
			O.R. 10. C.C.S. O.R – 7 O.R – 9.	
			I.O.R 5 C.C.S – 3 Duty – 2 Rem. 8.	
30-XII-17			Foll. reinforcements joined yesterday	
			#77320 Dr. Nathoo 7th A.B.C. –	
			77230 " Baldeo – do –	
			77228 " Mokham Singh do –	
			77364 " Mangal – do –	
			M.T.C.D. 8372 Waterman Chlorimuden S&T Corps	
			#9261 Br Sher Ali admitted Hosp.	
			#9236 Br. Latchman – 9th Coy. – discharged to duty.	
			Admitted. B.O.R – 2 Evac C.C.S 2 Rem. 8	
			I. Off. 1 " 1.	
			I.O.R. 4 – 2 Discharged 1. Rem. 9.	
31-XII-17			Admitted. Br. Off. 3 Evac C.C.S. Off. 2 Rem Off 1. C.R.S. O.R. 6	
			Br. O.R. 6 O.R 3 O.R. 2	

A5834 Wt. W4973/M687 750,000 8/16 D. D. & L. Ltd. Forms/C.2118/13.

Instructions regarding War Diaries and Intelligence Summaries are contained in F. S. Regs., Part II. and the Staff Manual respectively. Title pages will be prepared in manuscript.

WAR DIARY
or
INTELLIGENCE SUMMARY.

(Erase heading not required.)

Army Form C. 2118.

300

Place	Date	Hour	Summary of Events and Information	Remarks and references to Appendices
31 XII-17 (cont)			Disch. duty. ROR - 1. Rem. BOR - 2. I.O.R. Adm 4. Evac CCS - 1 Duty - 5. Rem VII (?) J R Hassard. Capt. RAMC	

A5834 Wt. W4973/M687 750,000 8/16 D. D. & L. Ltd. Forms/C.2118/13.

Army Form C. 2118

WAR DIARY
or
INTELLIGENCE SUMMARY.
(*Erase heading not required.*)

Instructions regarding War Diaries and Intelligence Summaries are contained in F. S. Regs., Part II. and the Staff Manual respectively. Title pages will be prepared in manuscript.

Place	Date	Hour	Summary of Events and Information	Remarks and references to Appendices
[illegible]	1.I.18		6 O R British adm 1 O R Br evacuated to C C S 1 O R evacuated Sick St 6 O R Brit remaining	
			11 " " Indian " 1 Off adm 1 Off + 2 O R Ind Evacuated 6 O R Ind remaining	
			Dr T4/259479 S T W A S C rejoined on discharge from hospital	
	2.I.18		2 Indians discharged duty 4 remaining 3 O R Br adm 2 Evacuated to C C S 7 remaining	
	3.I.18		Br O R adm 5 Evac 2 C C S 5 Evac to Corps rest St 5 remaining O R Indians Evac 1 to C C S 3 remaining	
			[illegible] FAZIYODIN 27th Lt Cav proceeded to Lucknow C F A for temp duty	
	4.I.18		No 1476 Ward orderly	
			Br O R adm 4 Evac 2 C C S remaining 7	
	5.I.18		O R Br Evacuated 4 to Corps rest St to duty 1 remaining 2 O R Indians adm [illegible]	
			transfer from No 3 C F A Evac 1 C C S to Lucknow C F A 1 remaining 3	
			No 473317 Pt SCOTCHER G RAMC proceeded to 13 Mech [illegible] for temp duty	
			No 104375 Pt HISCOCK H C RAMC joined for temp duty	
	6.I.18		O R Br adm 17 received on transfer from Lucknow C F A 8 Evac 2 C C S remaining 17	
			O R Ind adm 1 transferred to Lucknow C F A 3 1 to duty remaining nil	
	7.I.18		O R Br adm 4 transferred to Lucknow C F A 9 1 to [illegible] remaining 11	
			No T/34310 Dr PEACH B C A S C adm and Evac sick to C C S	
	8.I.18		O R Br adm 7 Evac to C C S 4 Lucknow C F A 5 Sick St 2 remaining 7	

[illegible signature]

A5834 Wt. W4973/M687 750,000 8/16 D. D. & L. Ltd. Forms/C.2118/13.

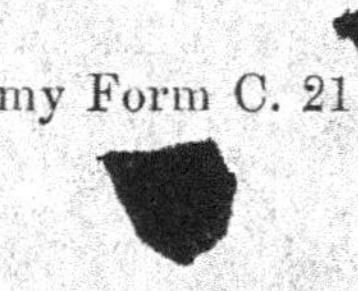

Army Form C. 2118

Instructions regarding War Diaries and Intelligence Summaries are contained in F. S. Regs., Part II. and the Staff Manual respectively. Title pages will be prepared in manuscript.

WAR DIARY
or
INTELLIGENCE SUMMARY.

(*Erase heading not required.*)

Place	Date	Hour	Summary of Events and Information	Remarks and references to Appendices
Field	8.7.18		Capt McCULLOUGH J C CAMC Joined from No 7 Canad CCA for temp duty	
	9.7.18		O R Br adm 1 Evac CCS 1 remaining 7	
			Capt ROSS D RAMC proceeded on leave to Rouen for 4 days.	
			SAS CVR PILLAI 29540 proceeded to U K for 10 days leave	
			No T4/059838 Dr TYSON F ASC adm hospital No 17458 Br R.F.A. ASC transferred sick to Lucknow CCA	
	10.7.18		O R Br adm 4 Evac Lucknow CCA 3 remaining 8	
			No 18 Cook PURSHOTHUM UPADHYA 2/2 Gurkhas transferred sick to Lucknow CCA	
	11.7.18		O R Br adm 3 Evac CCS 1 Off adm & Evac remaining 10	
			Capt L C JOHNSTON RAMC rejoined off leave & took over command from Capt F R HASSARD MC RAMC who rejoined Lucknow CCA	
	12.7.18		O R Br adm 1 Evac to Lucknow CCA 3 1 to duty remaining 6 1 Off adm & Evac	
			No M2/22571 Pt CACKETT W.T. MT ASC adm hospital	
			No M1/09276 Pt Wheeler SEARLE C ASC proceeded to 48 Mobile Workshops for temp duty. No T2/13232 Dr EDWARDS R ASC proceeded with water-cart to 2nd dismounted Div	S L J

Army Form C. 2118

WAR DIARY
or
INTELLIGENCE SUMMARY.
(Erase heading not required.)

Instructions regarding War Diaries and Intelligence Summaries are contained in F. S. Regs., Part II. and the Staff Manual respectively. Title pages will be prepared in manuscript.

Place	Date	Hour	Summary of Events and Information	Remarks and references to Appendices
Field	13.I.18		O R Br Adm 4 Evac to CCS 1 Sections St 1 remaining 8	
	14.I.18		O R Br adm 2 Duty 2 remaining 8. No 1871 SOWAR SUBGAN XX Deccan Horse joined in relief of No 1232 Br L/Naick TED SINGH XX Deccan Horse who rejoined his regiment. Lt Col FLEMMING AN DSO IMS rejoined from Div H.Q. on completion of duty as Offg ADMS and proceeded on months leave on	
	15.I.18		15.I.18 O R Br adm 3 Evac CCS 1 Duty 2 remaining 8. M T 4/059479 Dr GOTTS T.W. ASC was awarded 7 days CC for improper reply to N.C.O. No 9142 Br BHAGGOO ABC Evac to CFA with No 174855 Dr PIROO ABC rejoined from hospital	
	16.I.18		O R Br adm 6 Evac CCS 1 remaining 13. No 67092 Pt CONLON J RAMC proceeded to take over sick charge of Bdy baths in relief of No 134375 Pt HOSOCIR RAMC. The following joined unit to day M.T./34075 Dr LAYOCR ?L & M.T./ 027664 Dr REED G. ASC No IT Cook PARSHOTHUM UPADHYA 2/2 Gurkhas rejoined from hospital	
	17.I.18		O R Br adm 3 Evac CCS 1 remaining 15. 2 mules received from Remount. The following personnel proceeded to Lucknow CCS for temp duty No 413 Ward orderly ALI MOHD KHAN 12525 SARAN SINGH No 9223 Br NUR MOHOMAD No MT/2040 Sweeper KHACHARU	

A5834 Wt. W4973/M687 750,000 8/16 D. D. & L. Ltd. Forms/C.2118/13.

169

WAR DIARY
or
INTELLIGENCE SUMMARY.

(*Erase heading not required.*)

Army Form C. 2118.

Instructions regarding War Diaries and Intelligence Summaries are contained in F. S. Regs., Part II. and the Staff Manual respectively. Title pages will be prepared in manuscript.

Place	Date	Hour	Summary of Events and Information	Remarks and references to Appendices
Field	18.I.18		O.R. Br. adm 3 Off 1 adm & Evac to C.C.S. remaining 18	
	19.I.18		O.R. Br. adm 6 Evac to C.C.S. 3 Sialkot(?) 1 Lucknow C.F.A. 2 Duty 2 remaining 16 The following joined to-day from Workshops No. M2/121529 Pte SMITH A. M.T. A.S.C. & No. M/331549 Pte WIGGETT J. A.S.C.	
	20.I.18		O.R. Br. adm 13 Evac C.C.S. 5 Sialkot(?) 2 remaining 22 No. T3/024496 Dr ALDRIDGE E. A.S.C. proceeded for duty with 2 mules for temp duty with 2nd Dismounted Div S.A.S. C.V.R. PILLAI I.S.M.D. returned off leave	
	21.I.18		O.R. Br. adm 3 Evac C.C.S. 3 41st Hosp 1 Sialkot(?) 1 Lucknow C.F.A. 2 Duty 5 remaining 13 The following proceeded on 14 days leave to U.K. No. 14761 Sgt Maj ROBERTSON W. R.A.M.C. & [illegible] T/34075 Dr LAYCOCK L. A.S.C. No. 9203 Dr GOWPA(?) A.B.C. Evac to Lucknow C.F.A. sick	
	22.I.18		O.R. Br. adm 10 Evac C.C.S. 1 Sialkot(?) 2 remaining 20 Capt ROSS D. R.A.M.C. Evac to C.C.S. sick No. 77216 Dr NABI A.B.C. joined from Base No. 67092 Pte CONLON J. rejoined from English Cath[illegible]	
	23.I.18		O.R. Br. adm 5 Evac C.C.S. 2 Lucknow C.F.A. 4 Duty 2 One off adm & Evac to C.C.S. remaining 17	
	24.I.18		O.R. Br. adm 2 Lucknow C.F.A. 1 Duty 1 remaining 17 One off adm & Evac S.A.S. C.V.R. PILLAI I.S.M.D. proceeded with Mobile Amb to Dismounted reinforcements for temp duty. Capt McCULLOUGH J.E. R.A.M.C. returned to unit ~~[illegible]~~ on 23.I.18 and Capt HUNT J. R.A.M.C. joined for temp duty on same date with [illegible] & [illegible] [initials illegible]	

Instructions regarding War Diaries and Intelligence Summaries are contained in F. S. Regs., Part II. and the Staff Manual respectively. Title pages will be prepared in manuscript.

WAR DIARY
or
INTELLIGENCE SUMMARY.
(*Erase heading not required.*)

Army Form C. 2118.

Place	Date	Hour	Summary of Events and Information	Remarks and references to Appendices
Tull	25.I.18		O.R. British adm 6 Evacuated to CCS 3 Scabies Stn 1 Duty 5 Remaining 14	
	26.I.18		" " " 6 " " 1 " 9	
			O.R. British adm 2	
			O.R. Indian transferred from Mhow C.F.A. 4 Adm 4 Evacuated to CCS 8 Remaining Nil	
			No 1476 Ward orderly FUZIYUDDEN 27 S.C. & No 691 Ward orderly SARDAR SINGH XX D.H. rejoined from leave now C.F.A.	
			The following reinforcements joined & are taken on strength No 77243 Br SRICHAND No 7638 Br SITALA DIN SINGH No 7622 Br No 77303 Br SADDIQ KHAN No 9241 Br HANOO MANTHII ABC awarded DATA RAM 7th Coy ABC	
			12 strokes for making improper reply to a superior Officer Carried out by APM 5th Div.	
	27.I.18		O.R. adm British 2 Evac CCS 2 Scabies Stn 1 Remaining 8	
			O.R. Ind adm 4 Evac 4 No MS/3472 Pt BURROWS RASC proceeded on 10 days leave to U.K.	
	28.I.18		O.R. Br adm 1 Evac CCS 1 Remaining 8	
			O.R. Ind adm 1 & Evacuated to CCS No M2/032933 Pt TURNER G ASC rejoined from temp duty Cavalry Corps No T2/13232 Dr EDWARDS R & No T3/024796 Dr ALDRIDGE E ASC rejoined with 4 mules & Water cart	
	29.I.18		O.R. Br adm 2 Evac 1 Duty 1 Remaining 8 O.R. Ind adm & Evac 2	

A5834 Wt. W4973/M687 750,000 8/16 D. D. & L. Ltd. Forms/C.2118/13.

Instructions regarding War Diaries and Intelligence Summaries are contained in F. S. Regs., Part II. and the Staff Manual respectively. Title pages will be prepared in manuscript.

WAR DIARY
or
INTELLIGENCE SUMMARY.
(*Erase heading not required.*)

Army Form C. 2118.

Place	Date	Hour	Summary of Events and Information	Remarks and references to Appendices
Field	30.I.18		O.R. Br adm 5 Evacuated CCS 2 Transferred Lines C7A 5 Duty 2 Remaining 4	
			O.R. Br wounded adm 5 Evac 4 Died 1	
			No M1/075571 Pte SMITH C ASC with one motor Amb & No TS/E19 Dr ROBINS J R ASC with one Horse Amb proceeded for temp duty with 2/1 Cavalry Bde [illegible].	
			No T3/027654 Dr REED B ASC proceeded with 2 mules & water cart for temp duty with mounted brigade H.Q. No M1/01578 Pte Whalen SEARLE ASC rejoined from temp duty.	
			No DM2/154401 Pte MAIN A ASC & No M/331549 Pte WIGGETT J E ASC proceeded on 10 days leave to U.K.	
	31.I.18		O.R. Br adm 1 Evac CCS 1 Duty 4 Remaining Nil.	
			O.R. Ind adm 3 & Evac to CCS 3.	

S. G. Johnston Capt RAMC

A5834 Wt. W4973/M687 750,000 8/16 D. D. & L. Ltd. Forms/C.2118/13.

Feb. 1918.

Secunderabad Ind. Cav. F. A.

Army Form C. 2118.

Instructions regarding War Diaries and Intelligence Summaries are contained in F. S. Regs., Part II. and the Staff Manual respectively. Title pages will be prepared in manuscript.

WAR DIARY
or
INTELLIGENCE SUMMARY.
(Erase heading not required.)

Place	Date	Hour	Summary of Events and Information	Remarks and references to Appendices
Field	1.II.18		The Ambulance moved to back area billets at BOILLANCOURT.	
	2.II.18		The ambulance continued march to VIGNACOURT. The Ambulance commenced to-day to treat the Indian sick of Ambala Brigade as well as the whole of the Secunderabad Bgd.	
	3.II.18		The following reinforcements reported their arrival to-day & taken on strength. No 3190 L/N Br MUNSHI and No 33805 D/Br GANGA RAM both 3rd Coy ABC. P NA/3771 Cook MOHAN LALL LKO/1459 RIYASAT ALI both of S&T Corps.	
	5.II.18		No LKO/1459 RIYASAT ALI S&T Corps admitted to hospital sick & evac to [illegible] CCS. No 14761 Sgt Maj ROBERTSON. W RAMC rejoined off leave. No 77321 Br NATHO 7th Coy ABC admitted to hospital sick. No 41730 Pte BELL. A. RAMC joined for temp duty from 5th Cav Supply Col. No T/35173 Dr COURT. J.R. ASC proceeded on 14 days leave to U.K.	
	7.II.18		One riding horse evacuated to M.V.S.	
	8.II.18		No H6391 Corp COLLINS J.J. 7th H. was reprimanded for being absent without leave. No T/27071 S/Sgt AYLMER F. ASC admitted hospital sick. No 9219 Br DORARAISAMY 9th Coy ABC admitted to hospital sick.	
	9.II.18		No M/121529 Pte SMITH A. ASC MT admitted hospital sick.	

JRG

A5834 Wt. W4973/M687 750,000 8/16 D. D. & L. Ltd. Forms/C.2118/13.

Army Form C. 2118.

WAR DIARY

or

INTELLIGENCE SUMMARY.

(Erase heading not required.)

Instructions regarding War Diaries and Intelligence Summaries are contained in F. S. Regs., Part II. and the Staff Manual respectively. Title pages will be prepared in manuscript.

Place	Date	Hour	Summary of Events and Information	Remarks and references to Appendices
Field	9.II.18		Sub Cond TERRY C.E. S&T Corps proceeded on 8 days leave to Paris.	
			T/34175 Dr LAYCOCK A.S.C. rejoined off leave from U.K.	
			The following were severely reprimanded for being absent from billets No. 7111 L/Havildar TOTA RAM.	
			No. 3190 L/NAIK MUNSHI 3rd Coy ABC No. 9173 L/N GANGADEEN 9th Coy ABC No. 9226	
			L/N SIBDYAL 9th Coy ABC	
			No. T4/244571 Dr COWDEROY W. ASC & No. T2/13232 Dr EDWARDS F. ASC with 4 mules and	
			one G.S. Waggon returned to OC ASC 5th Cav Div, struck off strength	
			No. M2/223571 Pt CACKETT W.T. MT ASC was transferred from No. 7 CHA to Cav Corps rest stn on	
			7.II.18.	
	11.II.18		No. T/2TITI A/Sgt AYLMER F. ASC discharged from hospital. No. T4/059835 Dr TYSON	
			F. ASC proceeded to BEMES for temp duty with 2 mules & one water cart in relief of No. T3/	
			028154 Dr REED G. ASC on 11.II.18	
	12.II.18		The following proceeded to OC ASC 5th Cav Div in accordance with instructions received from OC ASC	
			dated 8.II.18 & struck off strength No. T/2TITI A/Sgt AYLMER F. No. T3/124996 Dr ALDRIDGE E	
			No. T/29122 Dr BAKER F. No. T/2T574 Dr CODDICK E. S.C. T/1167 Dr HILDING J. No. T/210265	
			Dr LEWIS T. No. T/34156 Dr LAWS W No. T3/028154 Dr REED G. all of A.S.C.	
			M/121529 Pt SMITH A MT ASC & Br DORAISAWMY 9th Coy ABC both discharged from hospital	

A5834 Wt. W4973/M687 750,000 8/16 D. D. & L. Ltd. Forms/C.2118/13.

Army Form C. 2118.

Instructions regarding War Diaries and Intelligence Summaries are contained in F. S. Regs., Part II. and the Staff Manual respectively. Title pages will be prepared in manuscript.

WAR DIARY
or
INTELLIGENCE SUMMARY.

(Erase heading not required.)

Place	Date	Hour	Summary of Events and Information	Remarks and references to Appendices
Field	13.II.18		M S/3482 Pte BURROWS R ASC MT rejoined off leave from U.K. One motor cycle No. 29873 received from Supply Col in place of one motor cycle evacuated to base. The following officers joined and are attached to unit. CAPT GILES J A RAMC Capt PLUMLEY R G G RAMC Capt O'CONNOR J P RAMC and Capt McCOWAN P G RAMC	
	15.II.18		No. 926 Dr SHER ALI ABC received 4 days extra guard for being late on parade M2/223571 Pte CACKETT evacuated sick from No 1 CCHA to No 41 St Hosp on 11.2.18 & struck off strength of ambulance. No. M2/050080 Pte MORGAN T E C ASC proceeded on 5 days leave to U.K.	
	16.II.18		Capt O'CONNOR J.P. RAMC posted to 5th Field Sq R.E. & struck off strength. No T/25172 Dr THORPE W ASC proceeded on 5 days leave to U.K. No. M2/223571 Pte CACKETT ASC rejoined from hospital & taken on strength. M/121529 Pte SMITH A admitted hospital sick. Capt HUNT J W CAMC returned to No 7 CCHA No 3190 L/N MUNSHI 2nd Cy ABC proceeded to [illegible] en route for INDIA.	
	17.II.18		No M2/081717 Pte DAVIES H ASC proceeded with motor Amb to Ambulance Bgd mounted sect for temp duty. The following returned off leave Lieut Col A N FLEMMING DSO IMS from U.K. Sub Cond TERRY S&T Corps from Paris. M/331549 Pte WIGGETT J S ASC from U.K. The following proceeded to Supply Col Workshops with 2 Wolseleys Amb & 1 Daimler Amb for exchange for 3 Sunbeam Ambs. of 3rd Cav Div. in accordance with instructions from O C ASC 5th Cav Div No M1/08547 Pte HUGH J No M/07571 Dr SMITH C No M/20452 Pte TEBBETT W T all ASC. S G Johnston Capt RAMC	J R G

A5834 Wt. W4973/M687 750,000 8/16 D. D. & L. Ltd. Forms/C.2118/13.

Army Form C. 2118.

Instructions regarding War Diaries and Intelligence Summaries are contained in F. S. Regs., Part II. and the Staff Manual respectively. Title pages will be prepared in manuscript.

WAR DIARY
INTELLIGENCE SUMMARY.
(Erase heading not required.)

Place	Date	Hour	Summary of Events and Information	Remarks and references to Appendices
VIGNACOURT	18.2.18	DM I	Took over command of the Ambulance from Capt L.C. Johnston R.A.M.C on return from base. O. L. Fleming Lt Col RAMC	
	23.2.18	DM II	A party of 33 Indians departed today to entrain for TARANTO en route to Egypt. Yesterday the ambulance paraded before the Cavalry Corps Commander who made a speech to the troops. 3 Sunbeam Motor Ambulances arrived from 3rd Cav Dn in place of 2 Wolseleys & one Sunbeam, with drivers complete. Capt. L. C. Johnston R.A.M.C. proceeded on 5 days leave to England. 6 ambulance horses were exchanged for mules with A.H.T. Co today.	OLF

Army Form C. 2118.

Instructions regarding War Diaries and Intelligence Summaries are contained in F. S. Regs., Part II. and the Staff Manual respectively. Title pages will be prepared in manuscript.

WAR DIARY

or

INTELLIGENCE SUMMARY.

(Erase heading not required.)

Place	Date	Hour	Summary of Events and Information	Remarks and references to Appendices
VIGNACOURT			104375 Pte Hiscock H.C. RAMC proceeded to 13 M.G.C. Squadron in relief of 473317 Pte Scriven G. RAMC rejoined Ambulance same day	
	23.2.18			
	24.2.18		7101 L/Hav Totaram 7th Co. A.S.C. and 8205 Naick Phool Singh 7th Co. A.S.C. and 31 bearers proceeded yesterday as advance party to [illegible] Saleux for Toronto	
			T4/059638 Dr Tyson E. A.S.C. rejoined yesterday with 2 mules and water cart from temporary duty with 34 Poona Horse	
			M2/055880 Pte Morgan T.F.C. A.S.C. rejoined from leave to U.K. yesterday	
	25.2.18		T/25672 Dr Thorpe W. A.S.C. rejoined from leave to UK this day	
			43653 Pte Lamb T. RAMC rejoined from temp duty from Supply Column this day	
	26.2.18		81538 Cpl Bailey J.W. RAMC proceeded on 14 days leave to U.K. yesterday	
			T4/059479 Dr Goots J.W. A.S.C. " " " " " " " "	
			One riding horse and 1 L.D. mule received yesterday from 13 Sq. M.G.C. and H.Q. Sec[illegible] Cav Brigade respectively	JRG

A5834 Wt. W4973/M687 750,000 8/16 D. D. & L. Ltd. Forms/C.2118/13.

Army Form C. 2118.

WAR DIARY
or
INTELLIGENCE SUMMARY.
(Erase heading not required.)

Instructions regarding War Diaries and Intelligence Summaries are contained in F. S. Regs., Part II. and the Staff Manual respectively. Title pages will be prepared in manuscript.

Place	Date	Hour	Summary of Events and Information	Remarks and references to Appendices
26.2.18 Cont'd			Capt Ross D. RAMC was evacuated (sick) to England (No 2 R.S Cross Hosp) on 22.2.18 and struck off strength accordingly from that date	
27.2.18			T3/869 Dr Robus J.R. A.S.C. proceeded on 5 days leave [illegible] yesterday	
			M2/228871 Pte Cackett W.T. A.S.C. } T/29131 L/Cpl Tapsell G. A.S.C. } Rejoined from Course [illegible]	
			The Field Ambulance marched from Vignacourt to Ferrieres and billeted there yesterday	
28.2.18			1597 Dr Ghazala 32nd Mule Corps joined for duty [illegible] Field Ambulance yesterday	
			M1/09276 Pte Whlr Sear F.C. A.S.C. proceeded for duty with H.T. Co 5th Cav Div on 27.2.18 and was struck off the strength of unit from that date	
			T4/024295 Cpl Whlr Congdon R. A.S.C. Joined for duty from A.H.T. [illegible] on 27.2.18 and was taken on strength of the unit [illegible] date	J McG

A5834 Wt. W4973/M687 750,000 8/16 D. D. & L. Ltd. Forms/C.2118/13.

Army Form C. 2118.

WAR DIARY
INTELLIGENCE SUMMARY.

(Erase heading not required.)

Instructions regarding War Diaries and Intelligence Summaries are contained in F. S. Regs., Part II. and the Staff Manual respectively. Title pages will be prepared in manuscript.

Place	Date	Hour	Summary of Events and Information	Remarks and references to Appendices
			Weekly sick state for the month	
			Admitted / to C.C.S. / transfers to C. F.A. / transfers to [illegible] F.A. / Remaining	
	1st		B.O.R. 3 / — / B.O.R. 3 / I.O.R. 3 / nil	
			I.O.R. 4 / I.O.R. 1	
	2nd		B.O.R. 1 / B.O.R. 1	
			I.O.R. 2 / I.O.R. 2	
	3rd		B.O. nil	
	4th		nil	B.O.R. 0
	5th		B.O.R. 0	I.O.R. 4
			I.O.R. 4	B.O.R. 1
	6th		B.O.R. 1 / I.O.R. 1	I.O.R. 5
			I.O.R. 2	B.O.R. 3
	7th		B.O.R. 2	I.O.R. 5
			I.O.R. 0 / Duty B.O.R. 1	B.O.R. 3
	8th		B.O.R. 1	I.O.R. 5
			I.O.R. 0	B.O.R. 5
	9th		B.O.R. 2	I.O.R. 8
			I.O.R. 3	B.O.R. 7
	10th		B.O.R. 2 / I.O.R. 1	I.O.R. 7
			I	

J.R.G.

A5834 Wt. W4973/M687 750,000 8/16 D. D. & L. Ltd. Forms/C.2118/13.

Army Form C. 2118.

Instructions regarding War Diaries and Intelligence Summaries are contained in F. S. Regs., Part II. and the Staff Manual respectively. Title pages will be prepared in manuscript.

WAR DIARY
or
INTELLIGENCE SUMMARY.

(*Erase heading not required.*)

Place	Date	Hour	Summary of Events and Information				Remarks and references to Appendices
			admitted	to C.C.S.	Duty	Remaining	
11th					2 B.O.R.	B.O.R 5	
			I.O.R 2			I.O.R 9	
12th			B.O.R 2		B.O.R 1	B.O.R 6	
			I.O.R nil			I.O.R 9	
13th			B.O.R 0 I.O.R 0		I.O.R 2	B.O.R 6 I.O.R 7	
14th			B.O.R 3 I.O.R 1	1 B.O.R.	I.O.R 2	B.O.R 8 I.O.R 6	
15			I.O.R 1	2 B.O.R.	B.O.R 1 I.O.R 1	B.O.R 5 I.O.R 6	
16						B.O.R 5 I.O.R 6	
17th			B.O.R 1 I.O.R 2		B.O.R 1 I.O.R 3	B.O.R 5 I.O.R 5	
19th			B.O.R 1			B.O.R 6 I.O.R 5	
19th						B.O.R 6 I.O.R 5	
20th			B.O.R 1	B.O.R 1		B.O.R 5 I.O.R 5	
21st			B.O.R 1 I.O.R 1	B.O. 1		B.O.R 7 I.O.R 6	
22nd			B.O.R 2 I.O.R 1	I.O.R 1		B.O.R 9 I.O.R 6	
23rd				B.O.R 2 I.O.R 2	B.O.R 2 I.O.R 4	B.O.R 5 I.O.R 6	
24th			— 0		— 1	— 5 —	
25th			— 1 0			— 6 —	
26th			— 1 —	B.O.R 4	B.O.R 4	— 0 I.O.R 4	
27th			— 2 I.O.R 4	B.O.R 1 I.O.R 4			
28th			— 1				

J A Giles Capt RAMC

A5834 Wt. W4973/M687 750,000 8/16 D. D. & L. Ltd. Forms/C.2118/13.

March 1918

Secunderabad Cav. F. A

Instructions regarding War Diaries and Intelligence Summaries are contained in F. S. Regs., Part II. and the Staff Manual respectively. Title pages will be prepared in manuscript.

Army Form C. 2118.

WAR DIARY
or
INTELLIGENCE SUMMARY.
(*Erase heading not required.*)

Place	Date	Hour	Summary of Events and Information	Remarks and references to Appendices
3.18			T4/12905 [illegible] C. A.S.C. } [illegible] in [illegible] 5th Cav Div	
			T/28838 [illegible] A.S.C. } [illegible] / [illegible]	
			T1/631 [illegible] A.S.C.	
			The above [illegible] Cav Div [illegible]	
			[illegible]	
			being [illegible] to establishment	
			The undermentioned [illegible]	
			1496 Sowar [illegible] 27th L Cav	
			~~[illegible]~~ 282 [illegible] Saran Singh 10th [illegible]	
			9223 [illegible]	
			MT/2040 [illegible]	
			395046 [illegible] T.F. [illegible] 5th Cav [illegible]	
			[illegible]	
			M5/3482 Pte [illegible] R.A.S.C. [illegible]	
			this day	
			T4/084295 [illegible]	

A5834 Wt. W4973/M687 750,000 8/16 D. D. & L. Ltd. Forms/C.2118/13.

Army Form C. 2118.

Instructions regarding War Diaries and Intelligence Summaries are contained in F. S. Regs., Part II. and the Staff Manual respectively. Title pages will be prepared in manuscript.

WAR DIARY
or
INTELLIGENCE SUMMARY.

(Erase heading not required.)

Place	Date	Hour	Summary of Events and Information	Remarks and references to Appendices
[illegible] 3.18 Cont.			Capt Hassan [illegible] R.A.M.C. joined yesterday for duty and was taken on the strength [illegible] [illegible] [illegible] 147 [illegible] Maj [illegible] [illegible] 2nd [illegible] [illegible] entrain at Saleux for Taranto [illegible] Egypt. Capt Harris [illegible] R.A.M.C. [illegible] to Saleux to entrain for Taranto en route to Egypt. Col Fleming D.S.O. I.M.S. proceeded to H.Q. [illegible] Cav Div to take temporary duty for A.D.M.S. on 27.2.18. Capt [illegible] R.A.M.C. assumed command of Ambulance during Col Fleming's absence 22.2.18.	
14.3.18 SALOUEL			Col. G. L. Fleming I.M.S. rejoined the ambulance [illegible] morning to SALOUEL. 3 Sunbeam Motor Ambulances, one Ford with Sergt. C. LEWENDON and 7 men entrained on 2nd. Capt. J. C. Johnston R.A.M.C. Sub conductor Terry with 33 B.O.R. & 80 [illegible] with all the animals & transport wagons of the unit entrained at SALEUX on 3rd. Capt. HURLEY R.A.M.C. with 6 O.R. R.A.M.C. joined [illegible] [illegible] & [illegible] C. to awaiting disposal.	Entrained [illegible]

A5834 Wt. W4973/M687 750,000 8/16 D. D. & L. Ltd. Forms/C.2118/13.

Army Form C. 2118.

Instructions regarding War Diaries and Intelligence Summaries are contained in F. S. Regs., Part II. and the Staff Manual respectively. Title pages will be prepared in manuscript.

WAR DIARY
or
INTELLIGENCE SUMMARY.

(*Erase heading not required.*)

Place	Date	Hour	Summary of Events and Information	Remarks and references to Appendices
Contd SALOUEL	14.3.18		Ptes 206749 G. MOORE R.A.M.C. & H. COTTON M/100016 R.A.M.C. joined from Divisional H.Q. on 3.3.18 and replaced No 5299 Cpl. DAVIES E. J. & No 36848 S/Cpl. Dr FREEMAN as surplus of MHOW C.F.A. The two latter were posted to Divisional H.Q. on that date. The surplus R.A.M.C. personnel of MHOW C.F.A. & 6th San. Sec. were transferred to S.M.O. LONGPRE Group on 5th.	
			Capt T.A. GILES R.A.M.C. proceeded for duty to A.D.M.S. 3rd Cav. Dn on 12.3.18	
			Pte TURNER G. M2/032933 A.S.C. placed under arrest & remanded for court martial for committing an offence against a civilian on 11th. Handed over to the A.P.M. for custody on the same day.	
	16.3.18		Pte G. TURNER M2/032933 A.S.C. tried by Field Gen. Court Martial at QUEVAUVILLERS today.	
			Pte No 23968 G. HUMBER A.S.C. & T/1821 Dr SOUTHWARD A.S.C. of MHOW C.F.A. attached temporarily on return from base. Pte MORTON G. O. A.S.C. M1/08229 temporarily attached from 4th Cav. Dn Supply Col.	
			Pte No M1/09658 HARRISON R. A.S.C. joined for duty as motor cyclist from 4th Cav. Dn Supply Col.	

(A7092). Wt. W12839/M1293. 75,0.0. 1/17. D. D. & L., Ltd. Forms/C.2118/14.

Army Form C. 2118.

Instructions regarding War Diaries and Intelligence Summaries are contained in F. S. Regs., Part II. and the Staff Manual respectively. Title pages will be prepared in manuscript.

WAR DIARY
or
INTELLIGENCE SUMMARY.
(Erase heading not required.)

Place	Date	Hour	Summary of Events and Information	Remarks and references to Appendices
19.3.18			The remainder of the unit entraining for MARSEILLES at SALEUX this morning	
22.3.18 MARSEILLES			arrived at MARSEILLES at 1.30 a.m. and proceeded to Camp LA VALENTINE –	
			Pte COLLINS E A.S.C. evacuated to hospital with fractured [illegible] on 21st	
			The motor ambulance cars (3) which arrived today went straight [illegible]	
			The animals with H.T. personnel have not yet embarked and are encamped also at LA VALENTINE	
			Ptes HUMBER & SOUTHWARD rejoined their unit. R	
23.3.18			one riding horse evacuated to MOB. Vet. Sec. today.	
31.3.18			Moved to No 10 camp on 24th. Pte S TURNER awarded 28 days Fd. punishment No 2 by Field Gen Court Martial	
			Pte MORTON A.S.C. returned to 4th Cav. Div. Supply Col.n on 25th	
			Capt. J.S. Johnston R.A.M.C. embarked on Caledonia on 28th and the following on the MENOMINEE	
			on 30th. No M1/09058 Pte Harrison R. A.S.C. S.W.O. Sardar Singh 691 Pte Jordan R.A.M.C. 67092	
			M/331549 Wiggett J. – Yar uddin 1476 – Lewis 42653	
			M2/150186 – Bridgwater B. S. Sarwan Singh 2825 embarked on Caledonia on 30th	
			M2/074831 Harris S. Syce Rachan [illegible] 2040 Salwan [illegible] 143	
			A. L. Fleming [illegible]	

(A7092). Wt. W12839/M1293. 75,000. 1/17. D. D. & L., Ltd. Forms/C.2118/14.

Army ~~Form~~ C. 2118.

Instructions regarding War Diaries and Intelligence Summaries are contained in F. S. Regs., Part II. and the Staff Manual respectively. Title pages will be prepared in manuscript.

WAR DIARY
or
~~INTELLIGENCE SUMMARY.~~
(Erase heading not required.)

Place	Date	Hour	Summary of Events and Information	Remarks and references to Appendices
		Apr 1918	Confidential War Diary SECUNDERABAD C. 7. A from 10.4.18 to 30.4.18	

A5834 Wt. W4973 M687 750,000 8/16 D. D. & L. Ltd. Forms/C.2118/13.

Instructions regarding War Diaries and Intelligence Summaries are contained in F. S. Regs., Part II. and the Staff Manual respectively. Title pages will be prepared in manuscript.

WAR DIARY
or
INTELLIGENCE SUMMARY.
(Erase heading not required.)

SECUNDERABAD

Army Form C. 2118.

Place	Date	Hour	Summary of Events and Information	Remarks and references to Appendices
MARSEILLES			Dr. T2/1966 HOUGHTON. J. A.S.C. evacuated sick with Gonorrhea on 1st.	
10.4.18			Dr. Botts T. W. T4/059479 A.S.C. & Dr. CONNOR T4/127687 C.O. A.S.C. awarded 7 days C.C. on 5.4.18 offence. absent from billets from 9 P.m. to 10.30 P.m.	
			The remainder of the unit will embark as follows.	
			~~Capt. [illegible]~~ Lt. Col. A. L. Fleming I.M.S. with 20 Indians & 65 animals on S.S. Maryland on 10th inst	
			35 B.O.R. on S.S. HUANCHACO on 11th inst	
			~~Lt. Col. A. L. Fleming IMS~~ Capt. McCowen R.A.M.C on 13th or 14th inst with one batman.	
			The following exchange occurred today.	
			Conductor L. E. TERRY & Sgt. cooks exchanged with conductor H. FULFORD Sgt. cooks	

(A7092). Wt W12839/M1293 75,0.0. 1/17. D. D. & L., Ltd. Forms/C.2118/14.

Instructions regarding War Diaries and Intelligence Summaries are contained in F. S. Regs., Part II. and the Staff Manual respectively. Title pages will be prepared in manuscript.

WAR DIARY
or
INTELLIGENCE SUMMARY.
(Erase heading not required.)

Army Form C. 2118.

Place	Date	Hour	Summary of Events and Information	Remarks and references to Appendices
			H.M.T. MARYLAND	
MARSEILLES	12.4.18		Troops embarked this morning. Details of 2nd Lancers 38th Central India Horse, G.S.B. Depôt Secunderabad Fld Ambce, Egyptian Labour Corps and other details including post office — in all 377 men 770 animals. Space for men is limited only on troop deck accommodating 306 men. The accommodation for warrant officers & Indian Officers. A small dispensary and a hospital for 5 patients, but the latter is being used for by Indian officers until wanted for sick. Cleared from the docks about 3 pm and proceeded to anchor outside.	
	14.4.18		Sailed at 1 pm. Inspected 2nd Lancers for venereal in the afternoon as well as for vaccination & anti typhoid inoculation. Fair weather. One other boat – HUANCHACO – in the convoy	
	16.4.18		Sea rough. A good deal of seasickness amongst the men. Inspected the rest of the men except Egyptian details as yesterday. The Captain inspected the ship to day. Found troop deck hampered with men's kits etc. Steps are being taken to remedy this.	

(A7092). Wt. W12839/M1293. 75,0.0. 1/17. D. D. & L., Ltd. Forms/C.2118/14.

Army Form C. 2118.

Instructions regarding War Diaries and Intelligence Summaries are contained in F. S. Regs., Part II. and the Staff Manual respectively. Title pages will be prepared in manuscript.

WAR DIARY or INTELLIGENCE SUMMARY.

(Erase heading not required.)

Place	Date	Hour	Summary of Events and Information	Remarks and references to Appendices
15.4.18 contd			Health except for seasickness good. One I.O. with fever and a syce suffering from mental derangement. He was drunk on embarking and has been in a condition of mania of a mild type since. Is better to-day.	
	16.4.18		A beautiful day & sea quite smooth. Men all exercised at morning parade. Egyptian details examined for venereal. In the whole ship one man found suffering from Gonorrhoea. Inoculated 10 men with T.A.B. antityphoid vaccine	
	17.4.18		Fine day, more wind, but not rough. Men exercised at parade. Arrangements made to have cresol sprayed on all horsedecks. Inoculated 10 men against typhoid and one officer (the CO). Two officers inoculated against cholera	
	18.4.18		Inoculated 10 men against typhoid & one officer; also 6 men & one officer against cholera. The ship is inspected by me daily. Sanitation is highly satisfactory. The syce under restraint has recovered & been sent back to duty to-day.	

(A7092). Wt. W12839/M1293. 75,0.0. 1/17. D. D. & L., Ltd. Forms/C.2118/14.

Army Form C. 2118.

WAR DIARY
or
INTELLIGENCE SUMMARY.
(Erase heading not required.)

Instructions regarding War Diaries and Intelligence Summaries are contained in F. S. Regs., Part II. and the Staff Manual respectively. Title pages will be prepared in manuscript.

Place	Date	Hour	Summary of Events and Information	Remarks and references to Appendices
	19.4.18		4 B.O.s inoculated against cholera & one against typhoid 13 men inoculated against typhoid	
	20.4.18		1 I.O. inoculated against cholera 6 men — " — — " — typhoid 5 — " — vaccinated Health throughout the voyage has been excellent. The men's rations have been ample except that the Indians have had no meat nor milk in lieu A. L. Fleming Lt Col IMS	
	21.4.18		Arrived at ALEXANDRIA at 11.20 am. Two sick one I.O. with Bronchitis & one P. Office detail with gonorrhoea to embarkation M.O. at 3.15 pm. Drugs & medical equipment handed over & key of dispensary given to chief officer A. L. Fleming Lt Col IMS	

(A7092) Wt W12839/M1293 75,0.0. 1/17. D. D. & L., Ltd. Forms/C.2118/14.

Army Form C. 2118.

Instructions regarding War Diaries and Intelligence Summaries are contained in F. S. Regs., Part II. and the Staff Manual respectively. Title pages will be prepared in manuscript.

WAR DIARY
or
INTELLIGENCE SUMMARY.
(Erase heading not required.)

Place	Date	Hour	Summary of Events and Information	Remarks and references to Appendices
ALEXANDRIA.	22.4.18		Landed ~~today~~ yesterday and entrained for TEL EL KEBIR at 1 p.m. Arrived TEL EL KEBIR about 8.30.	
	23.4.18		Remainder of the unit has joined up at this place. Hospital is open and has been for some time. About 100 patients being treated. 40 [illegible]. 5th Cav. Dn is being broken up and this unit is to proceed to Palestine to be attached to 7th Mounted Bde.	
	27.4.18		Marched to KASASSIN today. Dismounted personnel left behind to proceed later by train. March of 9 miles.	
	28.4.18		Marched to ISMAILIA 19 miles.	
	29.4.18		KANTARA 20 miles. A certain number of the [illegible] are suffering from breast galls.	
	30.4.18		Dismounted party arrived by train in the morning & the whole unit entrained for Belah at 1 p.m. reaching latter place about midnight. A. L. Fleming Lt. Col. MS	

(A7092). Wt. W12839/M1293. 75,0.0. 1/17. D. D. & L., Ltd. Forms/C.2118/14.

www.ingramcontent.com/pod-product-compliance
Lightning Source LLC
Chambersburg PA
CBHW081546160426
43191CB00011B/1851
9781474501262